RICHNESS OF MIND

Harness Mental Power
to Prosper and Attain Abundance

Robert B. Stone

Including excerpts coauthored by José Silva and Sidney Petrie

Copyright © 2021 Dennis Stone

Excerpts from "The Silva Mind Control Method for Getting Help from the Other Side" and "The Silva Mind Control Method for Business Managers" © 2020 by Jose Silva Royalties, Inc. and Dennis Stone, used by permission. All rights reserved. No part of this book may be reproduced or utilized in any form or by any means, electronic or mechanical, including photocopying, recording, or by any information storage and retrieval system, without permission in writing from the publisher. For inquiries, please contact Dennis Stone, txspaceguy@yahoo.com.

Cover art by Ayşe Ören.

CONTENTS

Title Page
Copyright
Introduction   1
Links to Books   2
Acknowledgments   3
Chapter 1 – From "The Magic of Psychotronic Power"   4
Chapter 2 -- From "The Power of Miracle Metaphysics"   24
Chapter 3 -- From "The Silva Mind Control Method for Getting Help from the Other Side"   40
Chapter 4 -- From "How to Gain Strength from Nature Sitting in Your Living Room"   46
Chapter 5 – From "Hypno-Cybernetics"   53
Chapter 6 -- From "Life Without Limits"   67
Chapter 7 -- From "The Complete Book of Life-Changing Affirmations"   81
Chapter 8 -- From "The Silva Mind Control Method for Business Managers"   83
Chapter 9 -- From "Celestial 911"   89

INTRODUCTION

My late father, Robert B. Stone, wrote many books to help people harness the vast powers of the mind to improve their lives, health, happiness, and success. Among many applications to real-life problems and goals, his books often discussed how to use these techniques to attain wealth and prosperity.

Indeed, only by starting with the mind can one reap the fruit of abundance.

The goal of this book is to gather my father's writings on this popular subject. Each section contains an excerpt of one of his books which describes how to improve one's fortunes in life.

Although the objective is similar in each section, the methods and tools vary. Much of this can be used immediately to help in your quest and I include a brief introduction to each section for context. In some cases, to fully put a method to work, some may find it helpful to read the cited book to more deeply understand and master the techniques presented.

I am very proud of how my father has helped so many people improve their lives, and I am glad that his works continue to do so. I sincerely hope that this anthology helps you achieve your goals and obtain prosperity and fulfillment.

Dennis Stone

LINKS TO BOOKS

Below are the books which are excerpted herein, listed by chapter. All are available in paperback and e-book editions. Several are available as audiobooks and you can hear excerpts of many on YouTube. For more information and a complete list of books by Robert B. Stone, please visit www.robertbstone.com.

1. The Magic of Psychotronic Power https://www.amazon.com/dp/B0722FNLZ9
2. The Power of Miracle Metaphysics https://www.amazon.com/dp/B08HQ7KYD6
3. The Silva Mind Control Method for Getting Help from the Other Side https://www.amazon.com/dp/B08JH4LMJ6
4. How to Gain Strength from Nature Sitting in Your Living Room https://www.amazon.com/dp/B01C7U3QS8
5. Hypno-Cybernetics https://www.amazon.com/dp/B08R3ZP229
6. Life Without Limits https://www.amazon.com/dp/B08J4274P5
7. The Complete Book of Life-Changing Affirmations https://www.amazon.com/dp/B01C6W6MEC
8. The Silva Mind Control Method for Business Managers https://www.amazon.com/dp/B08JH1BPPG
9. Celestial 911 https://www.amazon.com/dp/B08HQJ6LQ1

ACKNOWLEDGMENTS

Three of the chapters in this anthology were coauthored by dear colleagues of Robert B. Stone.

José Silva, founder of the Silva Method, coauthored two books excerpted here:

- "The Silva Mind Control Method for Getting Help from the Other Side"
- "The Silva Mind Control Method for Business Managers"

Stone and Silva coauthored other books together and Stone recorded several audio programs which teach the Silva Method. Stone often lectured on the Silva Method, introduced it into several countries around the world, and taught Silva graduates. For more information on the Silva Method, visit www.silvamethod.com.

Hypnotist Sidney Petrie coauthored "Hypno-Cybernetics." Stone and Petrie had a long collaboration producing many successful self-help books, the most famous of which was the best-selling diet "Martinis and Whipped Cream."

CHAPTER 1 – FROM "THE MAGIC OF PSYCHOTRONIC POWER"

Robert B. Stone characterized psychotronics as interaction between consciousness and matter. He wrote, "Picturing in the mind is the 'faucet' that turns on psychotronic energy." To help readers activate and focus their psychotronic power to address real problems, the book contains scores of "Action Plans" with clear and simple steps. Action plans about wealth are included here.

From Chapter 8: MIND OVER MONEY -- TURNING PSYCHOTRONIC POWER INTO MONEY POWER

In this chapter you learn to use the alpha (relaxed) level of mind to trigger a flow of limitless money into your life. Because psychotronic energy is at work, the money can come from many different directions. You learn to focus this energy on your business and cause steady improvement without limit, to climb the organizational ladder as high as you wish to go, to form new sources of income, as many as you wish. Finally, you learn how to tap information that can enable you double or triple your wealth.

A man from New Orleans has the uncanny ability to predict stock prices, commodity trends, and profitable investments. Ron Warmoth has helped hundreds to strike it rich in gold, oil and minerals by locating rich veins and drilling areas. In California he made six oil strikes worth 50 million for one client.

The Missoula Chapter of the Montana Mining Association used these words in a written testimonial to him: "Ron Warmoth does possess an unusual and unique ability to locate veins and deposits of minerals."

This unusual and unique ability is not one that Warmoth has trained or acquired. He claims that he was born with it and that he is, therefore, a natural psychic. This means he does not have to use an Action Plan to function mentally in amazing ways. "Let me see a map of the area," he says. Then in a moment, he points with his finger. "Here." And the minerals are there.

You and I are not born psychics, at least to the extent that Warmoth is. We need to develop the ability. To do this we need a system, a method.

A Chicago couple need money. They have just learned a method to function psychically—to detect information at a distance and to make things happen for survival. Money is a survival material. They decide to apply what they have learned to win a lottery.

They relax. They see themselves in a blue framed mirror with many problems. Then they change the frame of the mirror to white and see themselves winning a large amount of money in the lottery as their ticket number is chosen.

Each does this on his or her own. They repeat it several times a day for a week prior to the drawing. They win $300,000.

The method they use is a Silva Mind Control method. But it does not matter whether you follow a prescribed commercial method or a psychotronic engineer's method. The energy of consciousness is real energy and it delivers-especially money.

THE SUBCONSCIOUS MIND-COMPUTER EXTRAORDINARY

Dr. Douglas Dean of the Newark College of Engineering studied some five hundred successful businessmen and discovered they all rated high when tested on intuitive functioning. Many admitted to ignoring statistical reports and instead acting on strong hunches.

("Don't quote me on this. My stockholders may find out.")

The energy of thought is a very real creative energy. When you get right down to it, everything that man has created has indeed existed first at his thought level, usually in the form of mental pictures held while in a problem-solving mental "posture." It leads to sketches, diagrams, blueprints, working drawings, buildings.

Color it alpha.

Now that we see the tremendous amount of information that can be stored by a computer, we are beginning to understand the mind better.

The part of the mind that is not used in moment-to-moment awareness is called the subconscious mind. The subconscious mind has three main functions which we can now identify:

1. It keeps us alive.

2. It carries out instructions.

3. It stores data.

Keeping us alive means beating our heart, operating our lungs, digesting our food, and causing all of the systems in our body to function.

Our survival is linked to health, money and job, love, human relations.

Decisions regarding these matters come predominantly from the computer-like subconscious mind, even though we believe we are "thinking it over."

Past programming is what makes most decisions for us. We buy a certain kind of bread. We brush our teeth twice a day. We like a certain type of person. Past conditioning or programming can make us radiantly healthy, abundantly wealthy, and eminently successful.

It is also the cause of every curse known to man.

Positive suggestions accepted while at alpha level become a part of programmed behavior instantly.

A half century ago, Emil Coue had people in Europe and America look in the mirror and repeat over and over, "Every day in every way I am getting better and better." In time many had noticeable results.

However, he did not know about the alpha level of mind-the relaxed level.

At alpha you get immediate results. At this level of mind, the words or mental pictures go directly into the computer banks without any critical analysis, personal self-doubt, ands, ifs, or buts.

Instruct the mind to produce money and the brain neurons in charge of conscious thought begin inductive, deductive, and associative thinking processes.

The neurons that work below the level of conscious thinking begin their processes, too. They supplement the work of the conscious thought neurons, but they also are in touch with brain neurons in other people who might help to solve the problem.

Science is not sure, as of now, whether this is direct neuron communication or neuron-to universal consciousness-to neuron communication.

But to the utilizer of this psychotronic energy, it does not matter, any more than it matters to the flipper of a light switch whether the energy is coming from batteries behind the wall or an area generator miles away.

WHAT HAPPENS WHEN YOU INSTRUCT

THE MIND TO PRODUCE MONEY

For millennia man has been creating space in his own image.

There is a God, or gods, or Son of God. There are constellations that affect man's life. And down here on earth, there are gods of the volcano, of the ocean, of the trees, and of the rain.

The concept of God can place any philosophy into a tight religious framework. Maybe for the purposes of communication it would be best for us to free ourselves from the semantics of this and from stereotypes in speech or thought. Now, so freed, we can think in terms of space as an extension of ourselves.

Suppose you want to move something with your hand. To do so, you need your hand's permission. It does not withhold such permission unreasonably. But if it is broken or numb or has a valid reason, it will refuse.

Suppose space, as an arm of yourself, behaved similarly? This is a concept not too far removed from the God concept or the Edgar Mitchell continuum concept. As an arm of yourself, space would have to agree to act in your behalf. To get agreement from space you would have to "ask" or engineer that agreement in some other way.

Asking can be prayer. Engineering of consent, as Bemays defines public relations, can be picturing at the alpha level, *knowing* it to be so—a type of space relations.

There is one Oriental healer the writer knows who chants or prays to every saint that was canonized, every angel that was ever named, every prophet that ever lived, and asks for a healing. He touches all the bases. It takes him fifteen or twenty minutes—but people are healed.

There is a clue in this to contacting space or whatever space is itself permeated with. We give this space filler names—names of deities, angels, departed spirits. Maybe this has validity. But valid or not, this space filler becomes active with a consented-to wish, a consented-to prayer, a consented-to mental image. It is as if it is an arm of our consciousness.

Are you ready to ask "space" for abundance? Then you are ready to treat space as intelligent, logical, reasonable, cooperative.

This is the necessary attitude.

For the following Action Plan to be productive, you need to purify your consciousness of intellectual clutter, mundane pressures, and people problems. You need to be as pure as space itself in order to be attuned to it. This takes a Pre-Action Plan:

Pre-action plan for becoming space minded

Relax in a chair and breathe deeply.

Imagine all impurities leaving your body and consciousness with every exhalation.

Think of the space above where you are.

Go into that space instantly; imagine you can look back down at yourself sitting in the chair.

Continue this trip into space, past the coast, above the planet, past this solar system, out of the galaxy.

Feel love for this galaxy and all of the billions of galaxies "out there."

Return instantly the way you came, knowing you are in closer touch with space.

After completing this Pre-Action Plan, you are ready for the "main event," an Action Plan to win universal consent for abundance in your life.

Action plan to attract more money

Go to your "special room" and sit under the skylight.

Project your consciousness to outer space.

Talk out loud to space in a reasonable way, covering in a logical way:

> The nature of your money problem
>
> What amount of money would help you solve the problem
>
> Exactly what you will do with the money.
>
> *Use* your hands in talking and visualize the points you make in the "conversation."

Promise to give a sacrifice as a sign of your sincerity and respect.

End your session, knowing that at the moment of sacrifice, the money will be on its way to you.

Sacrifice by doing one or more of the following types of actions:

> Skip a meal, make a donation to a cause, feed some birds or animals.

WHY ALPHA HELPS MAKE PSYCHOTRONIC ENERGY PRODUCE BETTER FOR YOU

Why do mental images work better at the alpha level? "Why" is usually a wasteful question, but it might be of value to give this one a try. As we retreat from physical activity and from the beta world of sensory input, we get a step closer to the way we were when we were born a step closer to our source. This source of ours is really the space filler that acts as our extension. Maybe we have always been part of our source, part of the consciousness that fills space, and still are.

This is overly simple in its conceptualization and verbalization.

Actually, the truth is unfathomable because it is like an infant without depth and without dimension. When Jesus was asked, "What is truth?" he stood silent. His silence spoke more than cold words.

If we call the intelligence that permeates space the Infinite, and man the finite, then what life must be all about is that the Infinite is becoming conscious of itself through the finite. Or, as somebody once said, "God became man so man could become God."

Can it be that the thousands of years of man's philosophizing that there is a spiritual (nonmaterial and intelligent) basis to the universe as expressed in theological and metaphysical literature has not been in vain? We are consciousness. Our body is a place for consciousness to particularize, at a particularized plane we call the material world.

Our consciousness is energy, able to affect the energy we call matter, because it is closely "related." Our consciousness is really part of a larger Superconsciousness, or Cosmic Consciousness, which works with us if and when we get its consent. To get this consent we need to be in "touch." To be in touch, we need to be closer to it —at alpha.

HOW TO USE PSYCHOTRONIC POWER TO IMPROVE YOUR BUSINESS

Go to alpha. Visualize. Use your hands. Can you think of applications of this procedure that will help your business.

Alfred G. owned a shoe store. It was a marginal operation. Advertising did not seem to bring in more profit than it cost. Pedestrian traffic passing his store was fairly good, but they were the people who were on their way to or from work, intent on getting there.

He decided to use a triggering device to catch the attention of passersby. Did he use a flashing light? A revolving shoe display? An animated contraption? No, he used a tiny circular piece of red paper glued to the bottom of the store window.

Then he did some psychotronic work at home nightly: He went to his relaxed alpha level, entered his "special room," visualized the store window "wearing" the red circle, seeing people's attention called to it, and, if shoes were a need, their attention then turning to the shoes. At first there was no improvement. But he persisted for a week.

Then people began to stop in front of his window. Some came in.

Some of those who came in bought. Inside of another week he recorded a ten percent increase in his volume.

Sidney P. was an insurance salesman. He canvassed prospects obtained through newspaper advertisements offering free booklets.

His biggest problem was getting past the front door. People always had some excuse to ask him to "come back some other time.

He, too, harnessed psychotronic energy to improve his "prospecting."

Before starting out, he relaxed, went to his "special room" in his imagination. Then he saw himself being greeted at the door in a friendly way by people who needed his insurance services. He saw himself selecting the correct names and addresses for that evening's work-people who would be home and who would listen to his proposal.

Again, it took perseverance, but within a week Sidney P. began to see a difference. Nothing spectacular, but in his business, just one good contact an evening pays off. And it paid off well for him.

The difference in the approaches of the shoe retailer and the insurance salesman points up the need to adopt the application of psychotronic power in your business.

One basic procedure acts as the framework: You relax, moving into your alpha level of mind where brain waves slow down and become more synchronized with universal consciousness. Then you visualize your business activity in some constructive way. Here are some:

• A real estate agent sees "For Sale" signs change to "Sold."

- An artist sees his or her paintings radiating a light that touches people.

- A direct mail solicitor sees his own energy entering his mailing pieces and making them come "alive."

- A restaurant owner injects his food with "aliveness" and visualizes the tables filled as people are attracted to his "survival" fare.

- A taxi driver sees himself continuously in the right place at the right time for picking up fares and beating the traffic.

Calling the above "the adaptor," here is the Action Plan:

Action plan to improve your business

>*Relax* and go to your "special room."
>
>*Visualize* your business.
>
>*Use* "the adaptor."
>
>*End* your session, reminding yourself to repeat daily.

CLIMBING THE INCOME LADDER

George G. and I used to enjoy talking about numbers—like how, if the Indians had taken their twenty dollars when they sold Manhattan and invested it at compound interest, they might have more than Manhattan was worth today.

I did not know it then this was some twenty years ago—but George was doing some creative daydreaming about his own life, using numbers. He figured if he continued to get raises from the plastics company he was working for at the same rate as the past few years, he would be an old man by the time he had the kind of money he felt he was worth. On the other hand, if he changed jobs every few years and got a fifty percent increase each time he did so, he would soon be in great financial shape.

I began to wonder why George was changing positions so frequently.

He and his family kept moving—Pittsburgh, Cleveland, Boston. And his title became more and more impressive, like vice president in charge of sales. It was at our last meeting a couple of years ago that George told me of his job switch visions and how well they were working out. Then I told George about psychotronic energy and how he was using it in his creative daydreaming to activate his visions.

His reaction: "Nonsense—I'm just a good salesman for myself!"

There is a difference between daydreaming and creative daydreaming.

Seeing yourself wallowing in the lap of luxury is idle fantasy.

Seeing yourself taking specific actions leading to specific results is the application of psychotronic energy, especially if you are comfortably relaxed when you do it.

You can choose to climb the organizational ladder and attain more responsible, better paying positions in your present firm or you can decide instead, as George G. did, to climb the income ladder wherever it may lead.

Maria L. took a mind-controlling course that not only got her a good job in a school superintendent's office, but enabled her to become the personal secretary to the superintendent himself. Her images brought this about and she kept telling the superintendent about psychotronic energy and how picturing positively at the alpha level could solve some of his problems.

He just laughed this off and changed the subject. So, Maria decided to use her psychotronic energy to "get to him." She "saw" him going into a conference room. She stopped him to remind him of the power of positive picturing. She "saw" him listen, then he entered the room. She also "saw" him emerge happy.

Within a few days, the superintendent told Maria to prepare the conference room. Some parents were coming. It would be a difficult morning, he predicted. "It doesn't have to be," reminded

Maria.

"While I get the room ready, relax and see it all working out harmoniously."

When the conference got under way behind closed doors, Mana interrupted her typing to relax and hold the same images in her mind while in her "special room." In less than an hour, everybody emerged all smiles. The superintendent gave Maria a "thumbs up" sign. "It works!" he said. Later she got a raise, and he took the course.

Norman J. aspired to be a recording artist. He had a musical group. They practiced day in and day out. Occasionally they got a club date. Then Norman learned how to tap psychotronic energy. He went to his "special room" and "talked" to an imaginary recording company. Three weeks later, the head of a recording company "happened" to hear the group at a club appearance and gave them a recording contract.

Walter N., actor, wanted a role in *South Pacific,* about to open in a resort city where he loved to stay. He used his psychotronic techniques to see himself trying out for the second lead and getting it. He did.

Millennia ago, Hermes, deified by both Egyptian and Greeks, taught secrets that were so tightly kept that the term hermetically sealed still survives. One of the secrets was a practice that made dreams come true. It went like this:

> • Relax. Picture your goal accomplished. Take a deep breath and project this picture on to the air as it enters your lungs, knowing it will now enter every cell of your body.

The technique still works.

These are some of the myriads of ways that psychotronic energy works. It is activated by positive picturing at the alpha level.

All you need to do is decide on your goal and create the mental pictures that properly reflect it.

Remember, the picture you choose should not take something away from somebody else. Psychotronic energy so directed will be opposed, not only by the individual in question whose consciousness also has energy, but by universal consciousness working for the survival of everybody.

Decide before you perform the next Action Plan just what your picture or pictures will be. They are again called "the adaptor."

Action plan for a more lucrative livelihood

Relax and go to your "special room."

Visualize your present livelihood and the lifestyle it produces for you.

Use "the adaptor."

End your session.

Repeat once or twice per day.

CLIMBING THE ORGANIZATIONAL LADDER

If your decision is to remain in your present company and to move up in responsibility and pay, then the procedure is similar to the above, except your "adaptor" picture is in an internal organizational setting. In a way this is easier. There is more energy needed to move out and into another firm than is needed to move you up in the same firm.

However, the problem of treading on other toes becomes more of a controlling factor. Your "adaptor" image needs to be selected so as to invite the least amount of opposing psychotronic energy.

Simply put: Don't step on other people as you climb.

Remember Olga Worrell's work with the cloud chamber? When disbelieving physicists viewed the experiment, nothing happened.

The same is happening with similar observance of psychotronic phenomena by skeptical scientists. Things happen for scientists with expectant attitudes. If the expectation is that nothing will happen, very likely, nothing happens.

Your own expectations and belief are primary. But the resistance of another person's consciousness is also primary.

People do not need to stand in each other's way. Fear of the future, a poor self-image, and similar negative factors promote person-to-person competition where instead both would benefit by genuine person-to-person cooperation.

Do you see people standing in your way as you move up the organizational ladder? Or do you see them extending a helping hand to lift you up? The factor that makes the difference is whether your advancement promises to be a help to them or poses a threat.

Your advancement would help them if:

• Your skills benefit their performance.

• Your skills create new opportunities for them.

• Your presence adds beneficence to administration.

• Your increased responsibilities lessen their work.

• Your recognition by top management increases the chances for their recognition.

These types of changes enlist their psychotronic help. You can move ahead without their help, but you may not find your power of psychotronics anywhere near "miraculous" if theirs is in opposition to you.

The organizational chart is flexible. It can be altered to fit expediency.

You do not need to see a name removed from a box in order to see your name at that step in the chart.

You can add a box.

Action plan to move up the organizational ladder

Relax in your "special room."

Invite in key people one at a time and explain why you feel the company can benefit if you are given more responsibility and a better paying post.

Explain to people you may be by-passing, also one at a time, how you are no threat to them but how your advancement can be a boon to them ultimately.

End your session knowing there has been understanding and agreement.

Prepare physically an organizational chart showing a new box in it with your name on it in the appropriate "chain of command," division, department, etc.

Post it physically on the wall. Look at it frequently. Point to your box from time to time.

HOW TO OBTAIN VALUABLE INFORMATION INTUITIVELY

We are now getting into one of the most difficult to explain aspects of human functioning. Information comes to you. It is not your information. That is, you have never learned it or experienced it, researched it, or acquired it consciously. Yet, it proves to be correct information.

How did you get it? Can it be . . .

It's your inner voice?

It's your intuition?

It's your higher self?

It's the voice of the soul?

It's the voice of God?

Can you imagine any of the bespectacled scientists who are now daring to observe this in the laboratory, accepting any of these hypotheses?

In order to get "a handle" on just how we are able to pick up information by unorthodox means, it is helpful to know more about Cleve Backster, the polygraph specialist who found that plants react to people's thoughts. Backster took samples of his own blood and put them in separate containers. He put two silver electrodes into one of these containers, put the container in a shielded box, and hooked the electrode leads to an electroencephalograph. Whenever he thought of doing harm to one of the samples of blood, the other sample showed a violent reaction on the EEG.

Mary Baker Eddy would certainly nod knowingly at that. The founder of Christian Science knew the importance of positive thoughts on the well-being of the body.

But the real impact of Backster's experiment lies in the fact that cellular communication took place at a distance. Medical research explains the ability of the blood to call on various bodily resources when needed by saying such communication is handled by "chemistasis" or chemical messengers. These may exist, but there are direct communications, too, cell to cell, even over a 35-foot gap as in the Backster experiment.

Backster has also demonstrated that yogurt cells communicate over such distances. This was an automated demonstration with milk being fed to one batch of yogurt at a specific time and causing excitement on the EEG-measuring yogurt some fifty feet away.

Since Backster's work was announced, scientists all over the world have been working in this area. It is perhaps the field of research that is most demonstrative of the new discovery: the researcher is part of his own experiment. A plant reacts one way to Backster, another way to a scientist with a different attitude.

Consciousness cannot hide from consciousness. A cell's awareness, as minute as it is compared to man's awareness, is still there.

Your awareness as you read this book cannot be separated from the awareness of the cells of your body, from your family, pets, or plants. Should I say something especially loving that makes you feel mellow, your whole environment is affected. The opposite is true, too.

If an order is given to the neurons of your brain, "Urgent, need information to solve the following problem—competitors' product outselling ours; what can we do about it?" Those neurons will resonate with the information either in someone's brain miles away where that information resides or in the universal consciousness —and the answer will come.

It may come as a flash of insight.

It may come as a dream.

It may come through some "coincidence."

But come it will because the only requirement is a sincere desire.

That sincere desire is what causes the brain neurons to resonate at the necessary frequency, accurately.

There are ways to accelerate the delivery of that valuable information without waiting what might be days for the intuitive flash, dream or "coincidence."

Commercial mind courses teach the "mental screen" methodology which involves going to your mental laboratory, which is similar to your "special room" and seeing the required answer appear on an imaginary screen. This is quite effective but takes the kind of special training which these courses offer.

There is another way. It involves using symbology to induce the neurons to act within a specific time. One routine that is becoming increasingly popular is the tunnel technique:

Action plan to obtain strategic information

Imagine you are in a small boat entering a large tunnel.

Notice the pinpoint of light directly ahead; it is the other end of the tunnel.

Repeat the problem you have and know that you will have the answer by the time you reach the light.

Pretend you are drifting slowly along in the boat; feel its gentle rocking; hear the lapping waters; wait patiently for the answer.

Spend at least ten minutes on this boat ride aware of the monotony, occasionally repeating the problem, and knowing as the light at the end of the tunnel approaches your information will come.

Watch the pinpoint of light grow bigger as you approach the end of the tunnel.

End your session, emerging from the tunnel, knowing that if you do not already have the information, it is about to come.

Martin N. was a captain in the Marines and took a course in psychotronics which I gave at the Kaneohe Marine Corps Base in Hawaii.

I conducted the group in this Action Plan, not because any members had expressed the need for urgent answers, but just to demonstrate the methodology.

As I completed my monotonous monologue about "the lapping of the waters and the rocking of the boat" and reminded them that "the boat is now emerging from the tunnel," Captain N. jumped up and hurried out of the room.

We did not get the answer to why the sudden exit until the next session when he explained that his unit was in a competition that required complicated logistics. He asked for insight into this problem and as the tunnel exercise ended, a unique solution had popped into his mind that required immediate implementation. It proved to be the key to his unit's exemplary showing.

Another symbology that is also successful is going into a cave several times, first seeing pictures in the wall of your early life, then pictures of your present life, then of the situation you are in that needs an answer, and finally of the answer itself.

Or you can picture yourself standing in the front of a closed curtain. The answer to your problem is on the other side. State your problem. Request the answer. See the curtain rise, creating a small opening in front of you. The opening increases in size. Finally, it is large enough, and you step through—to the answer.

THE SECRET COMBINATION TO UNTOLD RICHES

This chapter started off with two Action Plans: the first, to become space minded; the second, to attract more money by getting the "agreement" of space.

That fact is significant.

It is as if there was a universal safe and there was no way to get at the real treasure unless you turned the dial in a special sequence.

Those first two Action Plans when used ahead of the subsequent Action Plans to improve your business or livelihood or get ahead on the organizational ladder, act as an "Open Sesame" to the universal store of riches.

You can storm the gates of that storehouse with physical energy alone, affirmations alone, and positive alpha picturing alone, but the results will be moderate compared to the flood that comes when you first become space minded and engineer the consent of universal consciousness.

If you belong to a religion, this does not conflict with its teachings.

You can in fact adapt the words used in these two "space" Action Plans so that they conform with your religious teachings. The concept of God can be substituted for space or for universal consciousness.

Also, the highest that a religion conceives—Jesus, Buddha, Mohammed—can be the intermediary in your behalf as you state your case.

The American Indians said, "The Great Spirit is everywhere."

By whatever name, universal consciousness, in which you live and have your being is all powerful—all rich. Those riches are your heritage. Activate your share.

CHAPTER 2 -- FROM "THE POWER OF MIRACLE METAPHYSICS"

A different set of tools is presented by Dr. Stone in this book. He writes, "It all starts with an easy-to-learn process known as alpha picturing—you learn it by sitting quietly in a chair and daydreaming in a special manner. It goes on to other just-as-easy applications of your conscious energy—the super physical, wonder-working energy that you have always had but never could quite control." The method is based on a two-step approach of deep relaxation and assured imaging.

From Chapter 6 -- How Miracle Metaphysics Attracts Wealth to You Faster Than You Can Spend It

Money is the symbol of abundance. The flow of money into and out of men's lives is probably, next to love, man's greatest concern.

This concern for money seems to have a strange effect: The rich get richer and the poor get poorer. This has been recognized even as far back as the writing of the Bible.

You can understand this apparent unfairness now that you have reached this chapter better than you probably could have understood it before you opened this book. You can see how a poor man who visualizes his lack and worries about his tomorrow, perpetuates that lack. While the rich man who mentally counts his wealth and anticipates its growth, perpetuates his abundance.

Change your habitual thinking from thoughts of limited money to thoughts of unlimited wealth and you change your life. However, this is not easily done. How can you think of wealth when you have more bills to pay than you have cash in the bank? How can you think of wealth when a note is due or the car is on its last legs?

Metaphysics enables you to turn the tide. This chapter contains the "white magic" of creating all the wealth you need.

How Pamela B. Used a Special One Dollar Bill to Start a Flow of Thousands of Dollars That Is Still Continuing

Mrs. Pamela B. was starting a metaphysical bookstore in Canada. She wrote me asking for any psychic support I could send her.

When I read the letter, I took a dollar bill out of my pocket and held it for a moment in my hand. I "saw" this dollar bill moving out into circulation creating an ever expanding stream of returning dollar bills.

"Good luck," I wrote her. "This dollar is not to be framed. Spend it for something right away and then watch what happens."

Two months later we met at a metaphysical conference. Her face lit up like a beacon when she spotted me. "That dollar bill," she reported, "has not stopped flowing yet. It's a miracle."

She told me how she gave it to a high school student for helping her place books on the shelves. The student told others about the "far out books" in her store. Clubs formed. Teachers called her in to describe her store to their classes. Students are now her best customers and bringing in their parents, too.

That dollar is still flooding her with more thousands of dollars today.

Later in this chapter, I will tell you how to energize money to create your own flood of cash. But first you have some mental work to do.

This is a world of abundance. Nature casts her seeds around as if they were going out of style. It takes one sperm to fertilize an egg. But is nature a piker? Have yourself a million.

Abundance seems to flow naturally through some people, but not through others. If you are in this latter group, I have some shocking news for you: a torrent of wealth has been ready to flow through your hands, but . . .you have been blocking it.

Here is how to get out of your own way and permit yourself to have all the money you need.

A Powerful Mantra That Materializes Money

Let's get inside Henry's head and listen to his thoughts. Henry is in between jobs.

"Five dollars has to last me until tomorrow . . . .What if the unemployment check is late? . . .I'll take her to the pizza parlor tonight . . . .Hope the gas holds out . . . I'll stay out until after the landlady goes to bed . . . .Hard to find a job . . . ."

Now let's get inside Fred's head and listen to his thoughts. Fred is in between his first and second million.

"Have to switch banks and get that higher interest rate. . . .Ought to start my own bank . . . .I'll give her a car for her birthday . . . .Never been to Bali, think I'll go . . . .Probably can open up some new markets in the Orient . . . ."

The pictures in Henry's head are free. True or false? False. Those pictures are costing Henry a fortune. It is the same kind of fortune that Fred is enjoying.

Well, you say, Henry and Fred are both picturing what they already have. True. But now for the good news: The picture comes first.

The choice of pictures is yours. You can have all the pictures of abundance you can imagine. The more you picture, the more abundant your life becomes.

Here's the hitch. It is next to impossible to think realistically of riches when your stomach is empty. And how can you visualize thousands in the bank when you just received a notice you're overdrawn?

What is needed first is a sort of mental aspirin—something to ease the pain of poverty so you can better visualize wealth.

Here is just what the doctor ordered—the "meta" physician, that is. Do it now.

Metaphysical Action Plan to Change from a Consciousness of Poverty to One of Wealth Using a Mantra of Abundance

1. Memorize these words: "Nature expresses abundance through me. I open myself to the flow of opportunity and wealth. OM. OM. OM." Pronounced as in "home."

2. Relax and picture yourself as wealthy. Let pictures of office, home, and family flow through your mind, reflecting dreams come true.

3. End by repeating the words you memorized in (1) three times.

This is an affirmation reinforced by a mantra. The affirmation is the part you memorized; the mantra the final word, "OM."

Let me explain OM. It is a sanctified sound. Sacred not because it is some particular culture's deity or blessing, but because it is the sound of nature herself! If all the spheres in the universe made a sound, if all the molecules vibrating in matter could be heard, if all the electrons rotating in atoms were audible, the sound would be like "singing" OM in a monotone.

Keep your lips open as you sound it. Feel how you vibrate to this sound. Everything resonates to this universal sound.

Test this out. Hold your hands out in front of you, palms down. Now sing "OM" in a low monotone. Can you "hear" the sound with the skin of your palms? Your palms tingle as it vibrates to the mantra.

The effect of OM on you is to open you to the universe. You become more aligned with universal flows of all kinds—the flow of order, growth, intelligence, harmony, and abundance.

The science of psychotronics, study of consciousness, is confirming the validity of ancient metaphysical prosperity practices. Where consciousness aligns itself with the universe, you automatically remove those private little dams you have built. And the natural flow of wealth enters your life.

The Wheel of Fortune and How to Make It Spin a Fortune for You

A state of consciousness is induced by the input of our senses. Sights and sounds of limited money are the main sensory input, but there are also the touch, taste and smell of limited money: the touch of worn-out carpeting, the taste of frankfurters and beans, the smell of musty wood.

Sight is by far the most important input. It is estimated that some 80% of our total environmental input is optical. That is why picturing is so important.

In the previous action plan, we used sight and sound. We need to do more having to do with sight. The ancients knew this. So they created the Wheel of Fortune. (See Plate III.)

Plate III

Found in many cultures, the wheel of fortune is symbolically the wheel of life. Although you may find one in some art reference book, it is best to draw your own, knowing that you are creating "avenues" for the flow of wealth with each spoke you draw.

There is a sign for OM. You are the hub of the wheel, the center of your universe. You can write the word "me." But the OM sign is a more powerful symbol to put at the center of your wheel of fortune. Label the spokes of the wheel with the qualities you aim for in your life, such as courage, honesty, generosity, compassion, strength, and so on.

Around the line you draw for the rim of the wheel, write your own affirmation of abundance. Here are some examples:

Spiritual affirmation. "The God power within me provides abundantly for all of my needs."

Scientific affirmation. "Money is energy. The more energy I put out, the more I receive. I grow in wealth."

Philosophical affirmation. "Abundance is Nature's way. I am an expression of Nature. I express abundance."

These should not be my affirmations. They should be your affirmations. Pick the kind you are most comfortable with. The spiritual kind is the most powerful.

Place the finished drawing of your wheel of fortune in some prominent place in your house so you see it frequently, even if only in a passing way. But before you do so, perform this metaphysical activation of it:

Metaphysical Action Plan for Energizing a Wheel of Fortune to Release a Continuous Flood of Wealth

> 1. Hold the sheet of paper with the wheel of fortune on it in your hand as you relax.
>
> 2. Place the wheel of fortune about six inches from your eyes while at the alpha level.
>
> 3. See the spokes as extending outward into every aspect of your life, reaping a crop of abundance and wealth that surges through you as you go forth.
>
> 4. End your session and post the wheel of fortune.

Your wheel of fortune is now a Wheel of Fortune.

You need not be conscious of it for it to work. If it is on the refrigerator door, every time you pass the refrigerator, you reinforce its power in you.

I have never heard of a case where the wheel of fortune did not work financial good in the life of its creator. Its effects may not be as dramatic as coming into a bundle of cash or inheriting an oil well. But everything becomes generally better for you as needs are met and financial limitations melt away.

How Steve B. Used Affirmation and Mantra to Crawl Out from Under a Pile of Bills into a Life of Ease

Steve B. had been married for ten years when his business went bankrupt leaving him with nothing but bills. The bank was threatening to foreclose on his home. The phone was cut off. The electric company was breathing down his neck. Bill collectors had stopped threatening and were serving summons. To get cash for food, Steve was kiting checks at the banks, an illegal procedure that was bound to catch up with him soon.

Steve had been interested in metaphysics, but now this passing interest became his last resort. He applied the affirmation of wealth in his life several times a day and sang the OM mantra. He also visualized himself free of his problems. Within three months he had renegotiated his mortgage with another bank, leaving him excess funds to pay all his bills. He had started a new business which was earning more than enough for his family, and he started to accumulate savings.

If you have used the OM mantra and created a wheel of fortune, you have changed the polarity of your consciousness. You are now able to perform amazing metaphysical money feats.

How to Energize a Dollar Bill to Multiply Manyfold Again and Again

At the beginning of this chapter, I told you the story of how I energized a dollar bill for Pamela B. and how it brought her a continuous flood of dollars. You are now able to create this same exciting phenomena—for yourself or for others.

I have seen this work for many people:

• A young man got an unexpected tax refund of $150 that same week.

• A woman found a $20 bill that same day.

• A writer got a $5,000 assignment in three weeks.

• A real estate woman, with no sale for months, made a $3,000 commission within three days.

How Mrs. Norma E. Made a $3,000 Commission with a Charged $1 Bill

Mrs. Norma E. was a moderately successful real estate agent. But sales had been few and far between for nearly a year. A seller's market had turned to a buyer's market and a large influx of new real estate agents were competing for the thinner market.

With three youngsters to feed and both a home and office to maintain, Mrs. E. was feeling very low when she came to me for metaphysical assistance. I had her put a dollar bill in front of her, and then had her relax and picture sunlight entering her body and then beaming out to the money from her solar plexus. She saw the money charged with energy so that when she spent it, it would return many-fold. She was the dollar triggering a deluge of dollars in her direction. Then she spent the dollar.

Three days after this exercise she received a call from a couple she showed a house to ten weeks before but who had decided to buy elsewhere.

"We're back," he said. "If that house is still available, well take it at the asking price." The sale meant a much needed $3,000 commission to Mrs. E. and a financial turn of events in her career.

Coincidence? Maybe. But metaphysicians certainly attract more than their share of happy "coincidences."

You have prepared your consciousness to accept unlimited abundance. You will now learn how to prepare a "triggering device" that can set off an explosion of wealth. That device is a dollar bill. It can also be a five, ten, or twenty. Wait until you have successes with these denominations before you use larger bills as your triggering device: Here is how to proceed:

Metaphysical Action Plan to Charge Up a Dollar Bill as a Triggering Device to Set Off an Explosion of Money

    1. Relax with the bill in your hand.

2. Visualize the sun above your head, beating down on you with brilliance and warmth.

3. See that sunlight entering your solar plexus (just above your navel.) Permit it to enter for a few minutes.

4. Now hold the dollar bill to your solar plexus. See it being charged by the sun's energy that you have stored.

5. When it appears to get hot in your hand, visualize yourself spending the bill and its energy touching off a flow of bills in your direction. See it continuing to do this wherever it goes.

6. End the session and spend the bill as quickly as possible.

How to Multiply the Deluge of Money by Combining Your Power with Others

Where consciousness goes, energy goes. I keep repeating this because it is *the* new concept of this age. The ancients knew it. But then mankind seemed to forget it. The energy of consciousness is now being rediscovered and harnessed to do work.

You energized a dollar bill (or higher denomination) to do work utilizing the energy of your consciousness. You used your consciousness as a battery.

Two batteries provide more energy than one. Three, of course, more than two.

You can build up the energy flow into a bill by working with your friends or members of your family. They must not oppose the action out of disbelief. This would short-circuit the energy. They must believe as you believe, do as you do:

Metaphysical Action Plan to Build Up Conscious Energy by Joining with Others

1. Review procedure as all sit in a circle.

2. Place one bill in center of circle. (Repeat the process later if more than one bill is to be energized.)

3. Clasp hands, left palms up, right palms down.

4. Proceed as in previous Action Plan.

Every philosopher and metaphysician knows that the universe does not give you something for nothing. But they also know that you have a huge credit built up with the universe because if you are like most people, you have been selling yourself short—accepting less money than you deserve for what you do, getting no money for many services you render, and thinking less of yourself and your worth than your true value.

So, the OM mantra, the wheel of fortune, and the metaphysical dollar bill are ways of opening your previously locked doors of consciousness and permitting the universe to pay its debt to you. This debt may run into the thousands of dollars or even hundreds of thousands of dollars. But then there comes a time when you must keep the flow going by building up your credit with the universe.

Before I set forth the procedure for building up this credit, let me review what you must do to keep your consciousness open to the money deluge.

• Repeat the OM mantra periodically.

• Keep a wheel of fortune in sight.

• Charge up a bill occasionally and send it out.

• Keep a bill of large proportions hidden on your person ($20, $50 —as in your clothing or purse or wallet compartment).

• Repeat the affirmation on the rim of your wheel of fortune several times a day.

How to Keep Money Flowing to You from Many Directions

Do you have a valuable gift or talent? Have you ever helped others to develop a similar talent? When writers freely help others to write, musicians help others to play, accountants give pointers to newcomers to their profession, good things happen to these good Samaritans. Since the person helped does not pay them, the universe must pay them.

When the universe pays you, it pays you much better than people pay you. Try it in the next few days. Do something of value for which you get no payment. Here are some possibilities:

- Help someone to learn English.
- Volunteer your time at a hospital.
- Join a fraternal or service organization.
- Write a letter to your editor or your congressman in favor of some reform.
- Read for the blind.
- Spend time at an orphanage.
- Be a companion to some lonely senior citizen.
- Help your neighbor with that planting or construction project.
- Stay overtime voluntarily to help the firm get a particular job done.

How is helping your neighbor, a friend, or your boss a metaphysical act? Try it and see.

First, you will receive gifts from people. Maybe they are not even the people you did something for. Accept these gifts graciously, knowing that these people are just playing a role of the universe. They have been moved to make you the recipient of their apple pie, the coconut from Jamaica, or the dress or suit they changed their mind about.

Second, good things will happen to you. Marcus Bach calls it serendipity. What is serendipity?

You may meet a person who has exactly the answer you need to move ahead on some project. Somebody you have forgotten about may return money you loaned him years ago. A magazine may accept a poem you sent them and enclose a check. The boss may invite you to dinner. These are all examples of serendipity—the universe's way of saying, "Thanks for joining the credit side of the ledger."

The real payment is still to come. The universe pays and pays, way beyond your personal sense of proper remuneration. When you give a book to a hospital library, it may be worth only $1, but the universe weighs more than the retail value of the book. How much is the thought of doing it worth? How much is the motive for bringing pleasure to others worth? How much is that pleasure enjoyed by these others worth?

A metaphysician knows that the wage scale of the universe is beyond belief. The metaphysician gives, gives, and gives, knowing that he is building up treasures beyond description.

You are now a metaphysician. Find out for yourself the real meaning behind the words, "It is better to give than to receive."

Far, far better.

Can You Discover the Ancient Secret of Turning Base Metals into Gold?

In India, a great wise man, Sai Baba, draws thousands to his ashram each day to listen to his teachings, receive his blessings, and observe him produce ash, gems, and gold jewelry, apparently out of the air.

I have personally discussed Sai Baba's abilities with scientists and lay people who have observed him close up. They say it cannot be trickery, but they have no explanation other than that he indeed does what he appears to do: materialize objects.

Sai Baba gives us a clue to the secret behind alchemy—the ability to turn base metals into gold. Perhaps it is not the base metal that is involved but pure consciousness.

Dr. Edgar Mitchell has observed materialization and dematerialization in the laboratory a number of times under fairly well-controlled conditions. If the present laws of thermodynamics were all he had to explain this, he comments, San Francisco should have been destroyed by the energy released.

But no energy was measurably released. So, something else was involved, which he is now working on.

L.W. deLaurence, whose books on the occult written some fifty years ago are still considered today among the most reliable, claims that the primary material used by alchemists was found within themselves. This then becomes their "philosopher's stone."

Sai Baba has been observed coughing up a stone the size of an egg on numerous occasions. But there has been no claim for these stones in connection with alchemy or materialization of other substances.

If deLaurence is carefully read, one sees a connection between soul essence and a watery mercurial substance which he infers can transmute impure metal into the purest gold and in sizable amounts.

In parts of Africa, it is said that there are "brokers" who enable you to sell your soul for cash. You approach these men and state how much money you need. They in turn tell you how long you may live. You return home and find the cash beneath a pillow or under a bed. Then at the agreed time, one or more years later, you are found dead of unknown causes. It is unthinkable for a civilized person to sell his soul for cash, but we do it, too, in our own way, as examination of crime records show.

All conjecture, true. But at the rate the occult is being de-occulted these days, the secrets of alchemy are likely to be discovered by somebody soon.

That somebody might be you.

Give the Universe Carte Blanche to Bestow Wealth Upon You

We are in the habit of thinking within limits.

We have undone the financial limitations we formerly placed on ourselves. Abundance can now flow into our life.

However, that habitual way of thinking in terms of limitations can still undercut our metaphysical action plans. The following is an example.

How Mrs. Evelyn V.'s Image of a New Home Backfired

Evelyn V. envied her neighbor across the street who lived in a much bigger house. She visualized herself living in that house. One night she woke up and found her house in flames. Her husband died in the fire. The house was destroyed, and all possessions lost. Her neighbor took her in. Thus, in this instance, her vision backfired because of her envy, and her limited vision.

A postal clerk I knew years ago asked me, "You mean to say all I have to do is relax, picture a check for a million dollars and I will get it?"

"Sure," I replied, "If that is really what you want."

A month later he greeted me excitedly with "It worked!" The check writing machine had been set wrong and there was a "1" in the million dollar spot in front of his monthly salary. Of course, the check was useless to him as it could not be legally cashed.

If the mind thinks in limited ways, the Universe replies in kind. How much better it is to give the Universe a free hand—carte blanche—in channeling wealth to us.

You are better off seeing *a* house instead of *her* house.

You are likely to receive more satisfying results seeing yourself prospering rather than prospering with this person's business or that person's know-how.

How Sam J. Won a $50,000 Lottery

Sam J. needed a grant from the government if he were to continue his research into the powers of the mind. However, instead of the money he received a "don't call us, we'll call you" type of turn down. Now ten years of hard work seemed about to go down the drain.

Sam had become an expert in alpha picturing. He relaxed deeply. He visualized his research not only continuing but expanding. Then he dreamed about a lottery ticket number.

One afternoon he had closed his laboratory and was about to go home when he met a friend.

"Let's cross the border and do shopping before the Mexican stores close," suggested the friend.

Sam agreed. They drove from their Texas town to the Mexican town in just a few minutes. While looking around a store, Sam spotted some lottery tickets. Among them was the number in his dream.

"These are my last few tickets," said the store owner. Sam bought them. A month later he was notified that he had won the equivalent of $50,000. His research was able to continue, and he bought some new alpha-measuring biofeedback equipment to expand it.

Let the universe decide how it will bestow its blessings on you. You must think wealth. You must think luxury. You must think abundance. You must think travel, possessions, cash in the bank. But let your thoughts be undetailed and unlimited.

Let it happen. It is yours to enjoy—without limit.

CHAPTER 3 -- FROM "THE SILVA MIND CONTROL METHOD FOR GETTING HELP FROM THE OTHER SIDE"

In this popular book, José Silva and Robert B. Stone collaborate to make the Silva Method work for everyone. It is a multi-week training program in one book. The key to the Silva Method is to enter the alpha level where brain waves are slowed. This permits access to right-brain activity to produce positive life results.

Using the Silva Method in Your Business

A chemical engineer is attempting to manufacture a synthetic blood vessel that the human body will not reject. After months of trial and error, he orders a dream to solve the problem. He dreams a formula, writes it down, and it is successful.

An insurance agent cannot get a return appointment to see a prime customer. He uses subjective communication to convince both the customer and the customer's protective secretary that it would be to the customer's advantage to see him. He calls on the company, is given an immediate appointment, and makes the sale.

A manager in a chain operation attends a high-level meeting of other managers in the chain. A difficult problem common to all is discussed—one of those damned-if-you-do-and-damned-if-you-don't situations. The manager puts his three fingers together and comes up with a proposal; it is unanimously accepted and proves successful.

Dream control, subjective communication, and the Three-Fingers Technique-are these the only applications of the Silva Method in business? No, every Silva Method technique has business applications. In this chapter we will identify the business applications for techniques, give you a brief roundup of these techniques, and at the same time open up new avenues for their use.

What about competition? I am frequently asked what happens when two people are programming for the same thing, such as selling competing products to a company; what determines who wins? If both are sincere and are programming with equal ability as to depth of alpha, mental picturing, and their expectation and belief, then it appears to me that the one who deserves it the most will succeed. The one who deserves it the most is the one who has the best record of correcting problems rather than causing them and of helping to make this a better world.

We earn merit by helping people, and by helping to correct problems on this planet of ours. It is something like people programming to win a lottery. Many people promise to give half of the money to charity if they win the lottery. But fail to see what is more important: what they have done previously with money they have already received.

Promises do not count as much as action. "By their fruits ye shall know them," says the Bible. We are judged by our actions, so if you take action right now to do all that you can to help make our world better, chances are you will be even more successful in the future, because you will have even more help from the other side.

The "Death Wish" and How to Eliminate It

B.J.'s father was a top government official in his country. B.J. himself was an extremely successful farmer, but then he decided to immigrate to the United States. In no time, he had become a rich entrepreneur, but he let somebody else run the company and that person milked the business of its assets.

B.J. then turned to real estate. He began to make sales. Then along came a sale of the sort most real estate people dream; it meant over a million dollars in commissions, but B.J. found himself making proposals that could only kill the transaction. It was then that he decided to take the Silva Method training, because he realized he had the equivalent of a "death wish" in business. He was used to programming for failure.

While at the alpha level, B.J. remembered his father calling him a good-for-nothing and similar names. He reprogrammed his own self-esteem and self-worth just in time to salvage the lucrative property sale.

People frequently feel that they do not really deserve the fruits of success. They unconsciously put up barriers to the recognition, the money, and the other rewards that success brings.

A poor self-image is like a prison of our own making; it is the concrete and mortar of parental put-downs, low marks at school, disappointing bank statements, and other limiting factors of the physical world.

Most people live their entire lives in that restrictive prison. But then somebody will take the Silva Method training and find that the prison door was never locked, and he can now walk out into a world of horizons of health, wealth, love, and joy.

How do you use the Silva Method to eliminate the "death wish" and other self-deprecating limitations? The answer is obviously to feel good about yourself, to feel worthy of abundance, and to feel you deserve the best in life.

A cartoon once showed a psychiatrist saying to a patient, "The reason you have an inferiority complex is that you are inferior." Only in a cartoon. We all have untapped potential awaiting discovery. The Silva Method helps it to surface. Here are several positive steps you can take now to accelerate that discovery and, in turn, accelerate your business success.

1. Do the self-forgiveness exercise again. Invite yourself into your peaceful place as you did before. Forgive yourself for all mistakes and apparent shortcomings.

2. Do as many of the "good guy" activities recommended in Chapter VII as possible. When you help others, you help yourself. You increase you feeling of deservedness.

3. Use the Mirror of the Mind. See yourself in the blue framed as you are now, not "making it." Erase the image. Move the mirror slightly to the left, change the frame to white, and see yourself as a successful business genius. From then on, whenever you are impatient or concerned see yourself as the epitome of success, framed in white.

4. Go to your alpha level daily and give yourself a positive affirmation, custom-built for your own situation, or use Silva's universally applicable one: "Every day in every way, I'm getting, better, better, and better."

More Ways to Get Business Help

Jack K. listened to soft classical music whenever he brought work home. Since they both preferred more popular music, his wife could not understand why. Neither could Jack—but he knew it helped his comprehension and retention. What Jack did not know was that the soft harmonies were stimulating his right brain hemisphere.

You have an even better way to stimulate your right brain—the alpha level. You will drift out as you read, but you can program yourself to keep functioning at alpha just by putting your three fingers together. Try to work the Three-Finger Technique into your business life. When writing a report, if you hit a roadblock, put your three fingers together and the way around it will come to you. If you have to speak before a group, put your three fingers together and your words will become more meaningful, and the right ideas will surface.

Going to alpha at your desk soon will no longer require deep breaths or countdowns. You need only defocus your eyes—taking them off visual stimuli by turning them slightly up—to trigger alpha. Daydreaming will also trigger alpha, and you will be creating your daydreams to solve problems.

Moments at alpha behind your desk can equal hours at beta. At alpha, you become a super-idea generator. That playful sign "Genius at Work" becomes a fact. You are able to be clairvoyant in wrestling with future contingencies, establishing inventories, making acquisitions, and handling day-to day snags. All the skills that I have just attributed to you are merely manifesting through you. You have an invisible means of support, an unseen partner.

When would you say that the two potentially most profitable minutes of the day might occur? The answer: when you put your feet on the floor in the morning. This is the start of the day for you, and it is the best time to program for a perfect day because you still relaxed, even sleepy. Sit on the side of the bed. Go to your alpha level in the usual way. See your place of business. Put a clock in the picture. It says eight o'clock, or whatever hour you start your business day. Play a mental movie. Everything is going smoothly; workers are in good spirits; the day is off to a good start.

Mentally turn the clock forward an hour. Your mental movie depicts continual progress—matters are ahead of schedule; new contacts are successful.

Continue moving the clock ahead hour by hour as mental movie shows fortuitous events, fruitful phone calls, and a perfect day.

These are the two most profitable minutes because they are creative of what you picture. They not only program you to make it so, but, because you are one via the other side with all the seemingly separate people in your day, they also program those others accordingly. We at Silva headquarters in Laredo, Texas, know it works. We do it.

Before a person can grow beautiful roses in his garden, that person must grow beautiful roses in his mind.

Before an architect can design an exquisite building, he must have an exquisite building in his mind.

Before an artist can produce an attractive painting, the artist must mentally see such a painting.

For an event to occur in the world of matter—your office, your store, your factory—it must happen first in the pictures of your mind.

CHAPTER 4 -- FROM "HOW TO GAIN STRENGTH FROM NATURE SITTING IN YOUR LIVING ROOM"

"The mind controls the body. By turning the mind to nature's scenes, you are attuning your mind, and therefore your body, to creation and therefore to life itself," wrote Robert B. Stone. This book uses visualizing the tranquility of nature as a powerful tool for right-brain activation and harnessing it to attain key life goals.

VISUALIZE NATURE'S ABUNDANCE COMING TO YOU

One of the greatest demonstrations of Nature's abundance fittingly comes from above.

We are not referring to the stars, although it is hard to beat them in terms of numbers. We were referring more to what falls on earth from above—seeds, blossoms, raindrops, hail, snowflakes.

All of these five examples are energy. An atom in a molecule of a petal, broken down, is energy. An atom is a molecule of water or snow or hail is energy. Money is energy.

In this guided imagery session, you will visualize a veritable blizzard of seeds, then blossoms, then raindrops, then hail, then snowflakes, then money. The blizzard of money will be activated by your spending at least a dollar in cash within 12 hours in another person's behalf.

This could be giving a gift, buying a child some educational items, or making change for someone who needs some singles. This spending of a kind dollar triggers the blizzard of money to arrive in your lap.

Of course, it will not fall from the sky, but it could arrive from some unexpected source.

Before you open your eyes at the end of the session, you will affirm prosperity and then you will be asked to enjoy an imaginary flower garden consisting of many different kinds of flowers in huge flower beds and adorning well-architected hillsides. Enjoy this mental movie for at least two minutes before opening your eyes and affirming aloud, "Universal Life Energy surges through me as I go forth."

Have a reader lead you through it, or make a recording with your own voice:

Sit in a comfortable position; close your eyes.

Take a deep breath and, as you exhale, be aware of how good it feels to relax.

Take another deep breath and, as you exhale, feel heavier in your chair.

Take a third deep breath and, as you exhale, feel a wave of relaxation go from your head to your toes.

Count backwards slowly from 5-to-1. Five, four, three, two, one.

Picture a beautiful rose garden.

Look closely at a red rose, then an orange rose, yellow rose, green rose, blue rose.

Imagine you are standing on an open porch looking out on a rural scene.

A gust of wind causes a shower of seeds to fly from a nearby tree. You are impressed by this natural affluence.

Another gust of wind causes a shower of petals from a nearby blossoming tree. You marvel at Nature's abundance.

A darkening of the sky brings rain. Wind blows the drops in a veritable blanket of rain. "See" this shower as a shower of Nature's energy which will help all growing things.

The temperature drops. Feel the chill in the air. The rain turns to ice. Sleet and hail fill the air without limit.

The temperature drops still more. Now snowflakes are falling. A gust of wind blows the flakes toward you in a veritable blizzard. "See" each snowflake as money flying in your direction.

Mentally "see" yourself spend a bill for some good and see the blizzard of money double in strength in your direction.

Mentally affirm, keeping your eyes closed, "I accept my financial condition as it is today as a temporary condition. I no longer put my creative energy into thinking of money shortage. Instead, I think of myself as prospering and rich. I see myself as the most valuable person I know. I expect more wealth in every way, every day."

Keeping your eyes closed, picture a magnificent flower garden. See beds of violets, bushes of roses; there are chrysanthemums, tulips, and daisies. Create this flower garden as if you were a landscape gardener. Spend at least two minutes creating it and admiring. You are on your own now. When you have finished loving the garden, count to five, open your eyes, and affirm aloud, "Universal Life Energy surges through me as I go forth."

Be sure to spend a dollar in somebody's behalf in the next 12 hours. You will then be eligible for a windfall.

WEALTH IS AN EXPRESSION OF THE

CREATOR'S LOVE FOR YOU

You are a product of Nature. As are we all. The abundance of Nature flows to and through you as it does universally, except when you block it.

How do you block it? You block it largely in three ways.

The main way is by separating yourself from Nature and/or the Creator. If you break the connection, the flow is stopped. More about how you do it in a moment. The second way is when you become a dead-end street for wealth.

The third way you block the flow of abundant energy through you is by worrying about your lack of money. You are using your creative mind to visualize and thus create poverty and shortage. We have already discussed this as the reason why the poor get poorer, so let's check out the first and second ways, the way you deny wealth by separating yourself from Nature and/or the Creator; and the way you become a dead-end street.

To explain the separation and the dead-end street, we have to shift to another language. As a scientist, I am frustrated because science has not had the courage to face the Creative Realm except to say that all creation started with the Big Bang.

The Big Bang falls flat on its face when you try to convince a small child. You then get some questions like, "Who lit the match?"

"What exploded?"

"Was there sound without air?"

All Creation started from Intelligence. And an Infinite Intelligence at that. What this Infinite Intelligence did to create the universe is so far out of the range of our intelligence that it is an egotistical circus to try and spell it out in an earth-language.

Let's start with an anonymous saying: "Within each being there resides a gem of purest light... Celebrate the gem that you are... Celebrate this earth and radiate your light to all the world."

In a way, this says what this book has taken six chapters to say.

The separation that prevents the flow of Nature's wealth, energy, money to you is your shading of your "light" from others and from the Creator. It is, in effect, a denial of the existence of the "light" in you. It is a denial of your divinity, your sacredness, your holiness. You exclude yourself, knowingly or unknowingly, from the family of God.

"There is no absolute truth," said a skeptic to me.

"Are you absolutely sure?" I asked.

Now about the dead-end street idea as an explanation of a second possible block.

Some years ago, an analysis was published of the lives of America's wealthiest man in terms of their state at death. All ten were either imprisoned, murdered, suicides or other tragic end. Had there been a love for humankind in their life, their final days would have been quite different.

If the money we receive goes into increasing our own accumulation of wealth, we are in effect a dead-end street for this expression of the Creator's love. We need to be a channel for this love, not a receptacle for it.

HOW YOUR MONEY CAN BE YOUR BEST FRIEND

If you live in the United States, the dollar bill has some important messages for you. Foreign money will not be discussed, but there are messages in much of that money, too.

Take a dollar bill from your purse, pocket or billfold and place it flat on your lap with the back of the bill containing the Great Seal facing up. Because this is your money and your country, its proclamations apply to you personally.

The motto on the Great Seal, on either side of the eagle's head, is "E Pluribus Unum," meaning "unity in diversity." One country out of many diverse states, but also one person - you - out of many different persons. You are special according to your dollar bill, and able to develop your sacred specialty to the fullest.

Also on the Great Seal, above the pyramid on the left, are the words "Annuit Coeptis." This means "favored our undertakings" inferring that there is divine guidance behind the country. That means, if you are in the United States, there is divine guidance behind you and your efforts to convert loneliness into togetherness.

Under the pyramid is a third affirmation, "Novus Ordo Seclorum," meaning "A New Order of the Ages." This refers to the destiny of the United States, but more importantly, at the moment, to your special mission on earth.

There were 13 states in 1776 forming the United States and you will find 13 stars above the eagle's head and in 12 other places such as in the number of arrows and other elements of the design. Think back -- Christ with his 12 disciples made 13. There are 12 signs of the Zodiac, plus the sun. King Arthur plus his 12 knights of the Round Table made 13. Thirteen is a powerful number. The dollar bill is a tender of energy; Nature's energy; the Creator's energy. Keep a dollar bill on you at all times.

But we are not finished. Note the top of the Pyramid. There in its apex is the all-seeing eye of the Creator. Note that the finial stone at the apex is not yet in place. The work of the country has yet to be completed. Your work, too. You have a great spiritual responsibility to finish your work.

And the eye of the Creator is on you—just as His eye is on the sparrow. You are being helped.

Remember the story which I believe was called "Footsteps in the Sand." A man walking through life alone saw two sets of footprints in the sand—his own and what must have been God's. This gave him great comfort. Then he went through a time of great trouble and trial. Looking back, there was only one set of footprints. He prayed, "God, why did you desert me?"

God replied, "I did not desert you. I was carrying you."

Your money is a symbol of the Creator.

CHAPTER 5 – FROM "HYPNO-CYBERNETICS"

In this book, Sidney Petrie and Robert B. Stone teach a simple but powerful three-step approach:

- *Step One – Relax comfortably*
- *Step Two – The Automatic Finger Signal. It is a way of knowing that your subconscious mind is ready to receive your Hypno-Cybernetic instructions. You should get the book to understand and use this powerful technical.*
- *Step Three – Give your subconscious mind instructions.*

The following discusses how to use step 3 of Hypno-Cybernetics for increasing wealth.

Step Three—Mining for Gold

The subconscious mind is a powerhouse, a genie, a gold mine—all in one. And it is even more.

Scientists are still not sure how it works. A waiter in a restaurant admires a house, stares at it longingly to and from work. One day an old lady finds him in the restaurant and offers to sell him the house at a ridiculously low price that he can afford. And there he is living in the house.

The images that we hold in our conscious mind long enough to etch into our subconscious mind come to fruition. The amazing part is how other people respond to help our own mental images to materialize. Does one subconscious mind contact another subconscious mind? Someday, perhaps, we will know.

But meanwhile, this we know for sure: the better the hypnotic contact we have with our subconscious mind, the more quickly and more effectively the conscious imaging is etched into it.

We have established that contact in Step Two.

Our subconscious is now ready to receive and act upon whatever we hold in our conscious mind. We can hold a statement in words. Or we can hold a visual image.

For example, if more money is your goal, you begin by saying to yourself the words, "I desire wealth and I will attain it." Or you can see yourself wealthy, that is, hold a mental image of yourself as a wealthy person.

The oral method is not aloud. You say and "feel" the words silently to yourself. The visual image is clear. You see yourself as you want to be.

How to End Your Money Problems with Hypno-Cybernetics

You are a creature of circumstance. True or false?

Absolutely false.

You are the creator of circumstance.

You are able to invite unwanted circumstances and suffer their arrival. Or you are able to invite the kind of circumstances you really long for and live up a storm when they arrive.

They say the rich get richer and the poor get poorer. They have been saying that since Biblical days. And it's true.

The reason it's true is that the rich are programmed for wealth.... They keep thinking how to increase those assets and how to increase that income. The poor are programmed for poverty.... They keep thinking of all the suffering that may lie ahead.

Knowing what you now know about the automatic mind, is there any wonder that rich people are paving the way for even more money and poor people are going to lose what little they have?

Somebody once theorized, that thousands of centuries ago, this planet was peopled from outer space with the purpose of playing a game called "limited love and limited money."

Who knows where this game originated, for a game it is.

There is no validity in poverty. This is a world of abundance. Poverty is the poor man's choice—consciously or unconsciously.

You can use H-C to change your programming from want to abundance. You can channel golden streams of wealth and glorious new happiness into your life.

Money is a measure of product or service supplied.

In order to receive money, you have to be productive. That is, you have to supply a product or a service. You can be a doctor, or you can be a service station attendant. Either way you are supplying a service. You can be a diamond cutter or work on an automotive assembly line. Either way you are supplying a product.

In order to gain in wealth, two things must happen. Productivity must be pushed up, and costs of living held down.

A woman's lib advocate recently addressed a university symposium. She called attention to the disproportionately low numbers of women in managerial positions. She attributed this to "outworn myths about women—myths that condition a woman to put limitations on her own expectations, to narrow her vision of the world, and what she might do in it."

Then she made her strongest point: "The really pernicious aspect of these myths is not that men believe them, but that women do."

When we believe in limitations we are believing in a myth. It turns out to be true, not because it was true all the time, but because our belief programmed us accordingly.

It follows that when we believe in our own capability to be productive and wealthy, we program ourselves to be just that.

People are constantly playing games connected with money.

The business tycoon often overeats, not because he has so much money to pay for food, but because he subconsciously makes a big stomach the symbol of "a big corporation" and affluence.

The woman who dresses gaudily can be exhibiting money frustration.

A man in Honolulu, who has been working in municipal sewers for 25 years, eats his lunch in the sewer and when he is on vacation from sewer cleaning, he takes a side job for a private contractor laying sewer lines.

And you've heard of the type who drives with car windows closed in the middle of summer to make you think he has air conditioning. Or the couple that runs out in wet bathing suits in the middle of winter to make you think they have an indoor pool. Legends perhaps, but nevertheless, indicative of the kind of money games people play.

However, the most common game is the game of limited ability to make the money you want. The pity is those who play it don't realize it is a game. Like some football players who start swinging, they get carried away by an illusion and think it's the real thing.

Abundance is the reality.

All we have to do is claim it.

How to Free Yourself of the Habit of Being Short of Cash

Mind control courses, under many names, are currently the "in" thing. They started in Texas, California, and New York and are now being given from coast to coast and in a score of foreign countries.

The main thrust of these courses is to operate consciously in the unconscious levels. Adults are being taught to examine the mental conditionings that now obstruct them. Of course, one of the major hang-ups is a feeling of limited self-worth.

If a person feels he is worthless, how can he or she develop a bulging wallet or bank account?

That negative conditioning or programming needs to be supplanted with a positive one.

Mr. S.C. was 56-years old. He was a very unhappy individual, never believing that he could do well at anything, make money or be respected. He had a lack of confidence and self-esteem. He had developed anxiety and tenseness. His attitude toward others was one of hostility and defiance.

Was Mr. S.C. affluent? Definitely not. How could such a man attract wealth?

He is now—because he changed his programming with H-C. His new instructions were to think positively, to know he could do whatever he wanted to do, and to have faith in his business judgement. Whereas he missed opportunities before because he was afraid to do what his mind told him to do, now he jumped in with confidence, accepted assignments, undertook new ventures. He calls H-C "the major reinforcement of my life." He is a relaxed, confident, and happy man.

You know you really don't need H-C to reprogram yourself. You can consciously think rich continuously over a period of time, and you will have acquired the habit of "abundance" thinking and the wealth will flow. It happens all the time.

Dick Jensen finally made it. The Sandwich Islands guitar player had a favorite daydream as a boy: by some sudden stroke of fortune, he would be booked to perform at the Copacabana nightclub in glittering New York. Fifteen years later his "impossible" dream came true.

But it happens quickly and effortlessly with H-C. No discipline. No remembering to catch yourself. No persistent daydreaming. No long period of erasing the old and substituting the new.

H-C gives you immediate access to that faithful computer of yours. The astronauts may do some of their own navigating but without their computers both in space and on the ground, they'd never make it.

Why don't you decide to "make it" right now? Start with cash. Then go on to bank accounts.

Here is how.

One of the great features of that mental computer of ours is its ability to utilize all of the previous information input in our combined experiences and translate it into a useful judgement in one particular area.

When you stop to think about that it is little short of miraculous. When you want to invest in a house, you consciously seek to recall what you have experienced in other house-buying or house-renting. experiences. But turn the job over to your subconscious, and the judgement is made on a thousand times that much information.

Turn the job over to your subconscious. That's the key. We have to learn how to get out of our own way.

Most people don't do that because they don't have enough trust in their automatic mental faculties.

This is really sad. They don't know what they're missing!

Are you ready to take a mental walk out of the world of the have nots and into the world of the haves? "Ready" means able to accept, as if it were true, a mental image of yourself as an entrepreneur, executive, or other post that involves money, responsibility, and the confidence to handle it.

"Ready" means a willingness to drop your present picture of yourself and concede that you have been wrong all this time. That is not easy to do. Nobody likes to give up a long-held belief. But the rewards are tremendous here and we hope you are not only ready but anxious to do this.

"Ready" means able to work up enthusiasm and, indeed, excitement over the new prospects that await you. "Ready" means more than you have faith that changes will come.

"Ready" means you know they are already on the way.

Get comfortable. Do your finger or hand levitation. When you get the signal that the wires are open to your subconscious mind, send these instructions: I see myself doing what makes me money. I see myself in the right places, with the right people, at the right time. I perform efficiently. I attract all the cash I need.

Ready? Go.

We want you to do this exercise again right now. But we feel that you can improve on the way that you just did it.

It's easy to say the words "I see myself." But unless somebody hits us with words like "sizzling steak," "dangling fish," or "glass of water," we do not usually go to the mental trouble of creating a mind picture.

This mental picturing is absolutely essential. It is what works the "magic." Can you see yourself behind a big desk? Can you picture yourself a key man or a key woman carrying out important responsibilities? Can you see others coming to you to get opinions, authorizations, instructions, approvals, advice?

Can you see yourself in a brief mental movie doing a particular job in a way that you've admired others doing it?

Can you see yourself with a big wad of cash, paying a restaurant bill with a fifty or cashing a monthly paycheck well up in four figures, not counting the cents portion?

These are the mental pictures that you need to use right now. Create three situations before you begin. These are situations you can see yourself in. Memorize them—one, two, and three. Resolve not to go on to two until you see one as if it were real, etc.

Set up your three mental pictures. Relax and begin.

Blocks That Can Stand in the Way of Your Prosperity

When a country suffers an economic setback, we call it a depression. The gross national product—that is, the total amount of goods and services produced—shrinks. Business people retrench. They cut down on expenses, reduce labor overhead, and exhibit little confidence in the future.

It soon becomes more than a business depression. People who lose their jobs are depressed. The industrialists who see their curve of sales nosedive are depressed. Proprietors of small businesses have trouble paying the rent and get depressed. And their landlords get depressed. And how do you think the President of the country feels? And Congress?

A British psychiatrist recently reported in the British Medical Journal that the amount of depression and suicide dropped sharply in Northern Ireland during 1971 and 1972, one of the bloodier periods of the civil war. Belfast, hardest hit by violence, showed the least incidence of mental depression, and County Down, the most peaceful area, the most. Psychiatrists have long theorized—and this seems to bear it out—that depression results when aggressive impulses are thwarted or inhibited.

The Fruits of Frustration—How They're Forced on You

What is the connection with money? Mental depression and its partner in poverty, economic depression, derive largely from thwarted or inhibited economic aggression.

We want to enjoy good things. But we can't.

We want to pay our bills, but we can't.

She wants that dress. But she doesn't have the money. He wants that car. But no chance.

The frustration brings mental depression. Mental depression perpetuates economic depression.

How do we end mental depression so we can enjoy prosperity? Avoid the frustration.

Canceling frustration from the present picture is easy with H-C.

Let's call frustration "Block No. 1." After we list the chief blocks to having all the money we want, well go to work with the right block busters.

Remember the shopping bag experiment you did? You closed your eyes, visualized a heavy load on your extended left arm and a light balloon pulling up your right arm. You opened your eyes and found that your arms had responded to this visual image.

Well, not only our body responds to our mental images, but somehow other people respond to our mental images and, eventually, the world of circumstances we live in seems to respond to these mental images.

To those who have always thought they were creatures of circumstances, it may now come as a shock to realize you are instead the creators of circumstances.

How to Control Frustration

What we hold in our mind's eye creates circumstances.

Is there any wonder that the person who keeps thinking about his dark today and darker tomorrow seldom sees the sun?

Like the weather, everybody talks about positive thinking, but nobody does anything about it.

When you picture the problem in your mind, your body, everybody, the world around you, generates that problem.

So, what do you do about it? Stop thinking? No. Start picturing the solution.

If you dwell on the problem, you are in there rooting for the problem, whether you want to or not.

If you would rather root for the other team, just dwell instead on the solution.

The rich get richer because they are always counting future profits in their self-gratifying minds. Can you imagine what would happen to the millionaire who kept imagining the worst?

And can you imagine what would happen to you if you kept imagining the best?

Put "negative imaging" down as Block No. 2.

Mr. L.R. was a moderately successful businessman, the president of his own small manufacturing company, and happily married to a charming wife. He was a rather unattractive, sloppily dressed, overweight man in his middle forties when he first came in for H-C assistance.

"I want to command more respect in my company," he explained. "Whenever I talk to an employee, I keep getting the feeling he's thinking, 'You stupid fat slob, who are you to tell me what to do?'"

L.R. recognized that these feelings were not reality rooted. But for as long as he felt them, he was interfering with his own effectiveness and undermining his own authority. Production and profits were not what they should be.

Use of a regression technique

At first H-C did not work. Attempts to reinforce L.R.'s own self-esteem, based on his competence in building the company and directing its success, did not seem to get anywhere.

Then a regression technique was used. L.R. was asked to put himself into communication with his subconscious mind via the finger levitation method. He was then asked to visualize himself talking to one of his employees and experiencing the feeling that such put-down thoughts were being leveled at him.

Then he was asked to travel back in time to the first time that he could recall experiencing similar feelings. He did this and then began to recall a time when he was in his late teens, enthusiastically talking about getting a date with a particular girl. He remembered his father telling him that such a pretty and bright young girl could have her choice of any number of dates. So why should she choose to go out with him? L.R. remembered he began to cry as he felt put-down by his father whose approval he was constantly trying to win.

Now the problem was easy to solve. H-C mental pictures were directed at reinforcing his knowledge that he was no longer a 17-year-old trying to get a date with a pretty girl, but that he was a man successfully married to a beautiful and charming wife whom he found very desirable and who he felt loved him as much as he loved her. He kept programming his automatic mind for a self-image of success at home and office.

A few such sessions and his self-worth rose high above such temporal matters as obesity and appearance, factors which could readily be changed. In a total of 27 H-C sessions over a period of a couple of months, the critical feeling at the office totally disappeared and was supplanted by one of competent authority.

Production rose. Profits increased. And as a side bonus, he lost 20 pounds and became style conscious.

Put your finger on self-worth as Block No. 3 to money in the bank.

As in the case of L.R., a block such as self-worth may be deeply rooted in some past experience. In a future chapter, we will elaborate on the "railroad" method of going back in time to remember such experiences and attack them with specific H-C reprogramming.

Meanwhile, you may not need to do this. We will assume you can gain significantly by removing these blocks via the direct approach. Later, you can attack specific deep rooted causes if they appear to be delaying the cash flow.

Block Busters That Let Loose a Flood of Wealth

The three blocks to a free flow of money in your direction are therefore:

Block No. 1 —Frustration

Block No. 2—Negative Imaging

Block No. 3—Self-Worth

They are in your automatic mind. They need to be removed and replaced.

Doctors still do not know how hypnotic effects actually come about. They watch as a hypnotized person is made to see, feel, and do remarkable things. But they cannot explain what they see. They watch as the hypnotized man creates a numbness in his hand until it can feel no pain. They listen as he talks readily about the past and his troubles' origins. They examine as symptoms of illnesses disappear on command.

But they cannot explain it.

They can only use it successfully.

How to Use Your H-C to Blast Roadblocks

You are now about to use H-C successfully to make you rich. It is like taking away the old blueprint that your mental factory is using and substituting a new blueprint.

The new product is "more money."

Now for the new blueprint, or more exactly-new programming.

Warning: This is like TNT. It is literally explosive in its effect. It can put you in a deluge of wealth before you are ready for it.

Some may prefer to put the book down right now and wait for a day or so while they accustom themselves to a new kind of future.

If so, see you later.

If you are ready to proceed now, here is Blockbuster No. 1.

Put the book down, do your finger rise exercise, and visualize as follows:

> I accept my financial condition as it is today as a temporary condition. I have no anxiety about it, I see myself happy. I am confident about tomorrow.

You can follow up in a few minutes with Blockbuster No. 2. Take a stretch. Get a cold drink.

As you drink the cold liquid, visualize yourself going from problem to solution.

Here is Blockbuster No. 2. Put the book down, relax, do your finger levitation, and picture as follows:

> I no longer put creative energy into problems. Instead, I visualize solutions. I no longer think of the little money I have. Instead, I think of myself as prospering and rich. I plan for a wealthy future.

The Final Blockbuster

In a few minutes you will be ready for the third Blockbuster. Take another stretch. Perhaps you'd like to finish that glass of water. As you swallow, think of yourself as gaining assets, instead of water, with every swallow you take.

Here is Blockbuster No. 3.

Put the book down, enter your blissful state of deep relaxation until you get the nod from your finger, then visualize:

> I am rich in experience, knowledge, talent, and capability. I see myself as the most valuable person I know. I see myself climbing the ladder of success to the top. That is where I know I belong.

An Instant Cash Bonus Builder

Want proof that something is at work for you right now?

We mean the kind of proof that you can spend now—green money.

If you have a problem about money and need some extra cash, here is how to get it quickly.

Relax, get the finger movement, and then think with expectation:

> My needs are supplied. I see myself with more money to solve a money problem. I don't need to know where it comes from. I just see that it has come!

Do it now.

Now stop thinking about the money problem. Start thinking about all money problems solved. Think about the solution. Do the three Blockbuster H-C exercises. Pause between them and get ready for a change each time. Accept a cash bonus right now by doing the final H-C exercise. Expect to have more money. You won't have long to wait.

CHAPTER 6 -- FROM "LIFE WITHOUT LIMITS"

In each chapter of "Life Without Limits," Robert B. Stone channels wisdom of a particular sage into – literally — sage advice to achieve life goals. The excerpts below are from Chapter 1, inspired by Chinese poet and philosopher Lo Fu, and Chapter 2 containing the wisdom of Druid priest Konedda.

How Good Begets Good in the Business World

We've established that good is contagious. So is bad. Take your pick. The choice is available to us every minute of every day, whether we are at home or away, at work or at play.

The business world is perhaps the most difficult environment in which to make that choice. The reason is that the good path is more likely to be less profitable than the bad, at least from an immediate point of view.

Attendance is lagging in your theater. You are losing money. Raise the price of tickets, you say. That sounds like the solution. So you do. And you make more money, but now some people find the movies too expensive. They stay home and watch television. Your gross take goes down instead of up. Does that mean next time you will know better? Don't bet on it.

You are in the food business. Lower quality costs less and you can make more. Your customers won't know the difference. So you supply lower quality. Your net profit jumps. But soon your customers are going across the street, where the quality is higher. At the end of the year, your lower volume of sales puts you in the red, while across the street there is a grocer who is all smiles.

Management and labor are constantly in a state of confrontation in the United States. Each wants a bigger portion of the pie. As a result, the consumer pays a bigger bill for products and services. Inflation becomes rampant, and everybody loses.

What would happen if both management and labor lived by the principle of not who is right, but what is right? How does one define "what is right"? Usually what is right means that which makes their world a better world to live in.

Now we are getting somewhere. Think about it. Is this the best of all possible worlds? Far from it. That means creation is nowhere near completion. Perhaps that is why the Creator has put us here—to help with the completion of creation.

Why Good Is Contagious in Any Activity

Anyone who thinks negatively is an ally of destruction rather than a friend of creation.

We cannot all be like that little boy who refused to leave the manure-filled barn. When asked why he kept digging in it, he replied, "With all this manure here, there must be a pony somewhere."

Still, it's easy to be positive. Anyone who thinks positively is an ally of creation. Such a person is a co-creator with the Creator. Help make this a better world to live in and you share the abundance that is already here.

You not only find that you are in a flow of money quite adequate to pay bills and buy what you'd like, but you are rich in the other aspects of abundance so essential to true prosperity: loving friends, romance, joy, and inner peace.

When you think positively, your actions reflect those positive thoughts. It is impossible to feel optimistic, supportive, constructive, and appreciative without actually being helpful, creative, loving, and contributory.

If you do something in your work that you are not really required to do, but it helps solve a problem, should you put in a charge for overtime?

If a visitor spots a book on a shelf in your living room, one you have already read, which your visitor is intrigued with, and which you decide to part with, do you charge your visitor a fair used-book price?

Your waiter is exemplary. He explains the menu, replaces an improperly prepared dish, advises you on desserts, and looks in on you to see if all is well. Do you leave him a generous tip?

There is a good reason not to charge for overtime; the same good reason not to charge for the book; and a good reason in favor of a higher than usual tip. That good reason is not to ingratiate yourself with your boss or with the visitor or with the waiter. It is to ingratiate yourself with the Creator.

You won't find why in any encyclopedia, book of knowledge, or compendium of wisdom. But it is carved in the stone of human experience: The Creator does not allow good to go unrewarded, and the rewards far exceed minimum wage.

Khahil Gibran, author of *The Prophet,* has said, in effect, don't invite rich people to your house for dinner. They will repay you by inviting you to their house for dinner. Invite poor people to your house for dinner. They cannot pay you back, so the universe must pay you back.

The universe is sure to pay you back. It is a law as immutable as the law of gravity.

This does not mean that businesses should give away their products or services. They would soon have to close their doors. That would be destructive, not creative. It would make this a lesser world to live in.

What it behooves you to give away are your favors and helpful acts both outside and inside of your livelihood. Sometimes it is better to charge for something that has been free. For instance ...

The chief librarian of a state-run Western university was faced with severe budget cuts because of a state revenue shortfall that affected all branches of the government, including this university. The librarian had been with the university for over ten years and had built up the library to where it was one of the most complete in the country.

Now he was faced with practically no new acquisitions, a reduction in periodicals, and shorter hours. Other department heads, faced with similar cuts, merely threw up their hands in surrender and said, "So be it." Not this librarian.

"I am a problem-solver, not a problem victim," he reminded himself and others. He made the plight of the library known and instituted a thirty dollar annual fee for the use of the library. Money poured in. Even people who never used the library paid their thirty dollar membership fee to support the library's excellent status. As a result, that university still has one of the best libraries in the country despite the budget cuts, thanks to a positive thinking problem-solver.

Step Off the Treadmill of Limited Money and Limited Love Now

The Druids were priests of the Celtic people, a race that included the Bretons, the Highlanders of Scotland, the Irish, the Welsh, and the Cornish. They idolized the oak tree as a symbol of the strength and prolific aspect of nature. And they were involved with the creation of Stonehenge in Britain, which remains to this day one of the more important legacies of the past. Located on the Salisbury Plain in southern England, it is considered to be mainly a monument to the rising sun, a marker for eclipses, and a source of other astrological observations.

They also built other stone circles, erected pillars, and created other megalithic shrines, including dolmens to hold their abundance of treasures, especially accumulated knowledge.

One legacy of the past has been lost in the complexity of the present. It is the legacy of abundance. Two ancient cities, lost for centuries, have recently been discovered that illustrate this abundance in breathtaking ways. One is located in Jordan, now hidden by narrow canyons and rockslides but still exhibiting styles of architecture borrowed from the dominant European cultures of the time. It is breathtaking in the vastness of its halls and rooms, all chiseled from the rock cliffs, and all adorned with an abundance of time-consuming and time-tested art.

The other ancient city has been recently found in the dense forests of Peru, about fifty miles northwest of Cuzco. Buried for centuries by the vines, trees, and dense undergrowth of the Andes mountains, it was named Machu Picchu and was both the greatest metropolis and strongest fortress of its time. To try to construct an equivalent citadel today would tax the wealth of the entire civilized world.

Neither of these cities are associated with the Druids, but they are examples of how a legacy of abundance such as that of the Druids can remain hidden from us.

The Druids, the Oak Tree, and You

The Druids worshipped the oak tree not only for its strength and abundance of its seed, the acorn, but for the understanding it gave them of the meaning of life.

Life is an endless chain. Should the oak ever be felled, it lives on in the many oaks that grow from its seed. The oak tree was never born and it therefore never dies. So it is with humankind. Life is an endless chain of experiences with no beginning and no end.

And, therefore, with no natural limitations.

But there are unnatural limitations. These are the limitations unnatural to the intelligence that runs the limitless universe but natural to the human mind.

We suffer from unnatural limitations. These limitations are caused by our thoughts. What we believe to be limited becomes limited in our life.

Nobody will argue with the fact that, in this life, we have limited money and limited love. Still, it is not true. Most of us who live this life make it true.

There is no limit to the money anyone can have. But because their name is not Bates, or Forbes, or Perot, or Rockefeller, they think they have been born into a world of limited income and limited wealth.

There is no limit to the love anyone can have. But because when they look in the mirror they don't see a Monroe or a Garbo, a Peck or a Cooper, they think that they have been born into a world of limited mutual attraction, and therefore of limited love.

Suffering from limited money or limited love is needless suffering. Your suffering is caused by your thoughts. Change your thoughts and you change your life. Here is how to make these changes.

How to Profit from a Druid Secret

The Druid priest Konedda was no ordinary person. As a Celt he appreciated the extraordinary

capabilities of the Celtic women, who knew how to draw on the limitless power of the Goddess within. She had wisdom, self-confidence, and magical strength.

Today, Celtic music survives and bears more than a hint of that ancient wisdom. In fact, Celts today see in that music a promise of a Celtic tomorrow—a resurgence of Celtic magic and the limitless life that it promises.

As spiritual leaders of the Celts, the Druids were considered to be the magicians and sages of their day. They were the masters of enchantment, the diviners of love. But their essential function was sustaining the prosperity of tribe and land. They did this by what was then considered to be magical means.

However, it was less magic than mental, a means that Jesus had taught centuries earlier but was little perceived and less perpetuated. It was a special use of the mind. Jesus put it this way: Go to the kingdom of heaven within, function within God's righteousness, and all things will come unto you.

Translated into contemporary language, Jesus was saying, in effect: Go within through meditation. Imagine money problems solved, health restored, creative goals reached. And what-ever you so imagine will come to pass.

In the days of the Druids, the individual power was looked up to. To share the creative ability of the mind with the common people was to give up your power over them. Of course, today the de-occulting of the occult is well underway. Millions of people, perhaps billions, already know the creative power of thinking.

Why, then, do they not use it? Why do they suffer from lack of money and why do they stifle their desire for love? Yes, I am talking to you.

The answer lies in the hypnotic power of the material world to monopolize your senses and to program your consciousness.

Limited space and limited time spawns in you limited thoughts and a limited life. Thoughts of limitation bring you limited love and limited ability. You build a prison of limitation for yourself. In the next five minutes, you will find that the prison door was never locked.

You will open it and emerge into a bright new world of untold riches and fabulous love. This will happen because two quick demonstrations will convince you that your mind is capable of more than you thought. You will change your mind about your mind.

This will start with your mind's control over your body. By seeing this happen in real life, you will open the way for your mind to continue its creative ability beyond your body—to your bed and to your bank account.

Two Exercises that Begin to Open the Door

The first exercise involves your arms. Read the instructions twice, then do it.

Exercise #1

Standing, hold both arms straight out in front of you, palms down, your arms parallel to the floor. Close your eyes. Imagine a heavy shopping bag full of groceries hanging from your right wrist. Imagine it being so heavy that you can hardly hold it. Imagine a big balloon pulling up on your left wrist. Make these mental pictures real. After a few seconds, open your eyes.

Read the instructions a second time. Done? Okay. Stop reading here, and do the exercise.

When you closed your eyes, your arms were at the same height. Now the right arm is lower than the left. Why?

The second exercise is best done seated. Read the instructions twice, then do it.

Exercise #2

Turn your head to the left as far as it will comfortably go and remember how far that was. Close your eyes and imagine that you are able to turn your head much farther than you did. Open your eyes and once again turn your head to the left.

Read the instructions a second time. Stop reading here. Do it.

When you turned your head to the left for the second time, it went a bit farther than the first time. Why?

The answer to both "whys" is: Your mind controls your body.

Do you realize what this means?

For starters, it means that you can make yourself sick and you can make yourself well. It means, too, that you can tap all the energy you need for whatever you need to do. It means you can develop skills and talents you never believed could be yours.

As a next step, you will learn that science has found that all our minds are connected to each other. That concept is indeed a quantum leap for the mind.

Do you realize what this means?

Eventually, on these pages, you will learn that thought is creative energy and that wealth, also being energy, can be created by thought as well.

And do you realize what this means?

Everett was fortunate to go to college but unfortunate in not being able to finish. The son of a Kentucky farmer who had saved enough in the good years to be able to afford his son's tuition for a little while, Everett found himself back on the farm after a year in a state university.

His taste of higher education made him bitter, and it gave him a feeling of inferiority. It intensified the belief that this was a world of "haves" and "have-nots," and that he was destined to remain in the latter group.

For a while, he drove a school bus, but was found to have liquor on his breath one working day and was discharged. He used his earnings to buy a used truck and help farmers with their cartage. His mother died and, one year later, his father did too. Now he was too busy with the farm to earn trucking money. He lived on his own produce and sold the surplus.

How is Everett doing now? "Haven't heard. I don't believe he has the money for postage."

The poor get poorer because the hypnotic effect of the limitations of the material world are just too dominant to be considered beatable.

Take, by contrast, Eugene. He was born in Westchester County, New York, a wealthy suburb of New York City. His father, a bank vice president, talked money at home constantly. The family enjoyed all the luxuries they wanted, traveled abroad with Eugene and his sister, and sent them both to the best universities.

When Eugene graduated, he disappointed his father by refusing to take a job in that same bank. He was sure that a life of abundance was his for the asking, free of paternal supervision. Instead, he joined an investment firm. His optimistic attitude won him client after client. His choice of investments proved magical. Everything he touched seemed to turn to gold.

Eugene married and lived in Southampton, Long Island, where his family grew to five children. His father remained paternal, but Eugene let his advice bounce off him. He was his own entrepreneur, and the world had no limitations. The last I knew about Eugene was seeing his name on the Fortune 500 list.

The rich get richer because they do not believe in any limitations in the material world.

Poor or Rich —The Choice Is Yours

The Druids were rich. They were rich because they made the choice to be rich and, once they made that choice, they knew how to manifest richness. They taught one another but seldom divulged their mental methods to outsiders. Today all we really know is that they attracted gifts from persons of every rank.

Each knew their relationship to the abundant universe early in life. This basic identity, when formed early in life, can remain essentially unchanged throughout life. The poor stay poor. The rich stay rich. Riches can be attracted to you in the form of friendships, joy, belongings, and, yes, even cash.

Occasionally, a life trauma of major proportions can alter these deep subconscious beliefs. A loss, an illness, a divorce, an incarceration can make a change in a person's subconscious beliefs in either direction. When the direction is positive, the event is usually referred to as enlightenment, or being "born again." In Japan, it would be called "Satori," in India "Samadhi."

Even a major trauma may not affect a person strongly enough to move him or her from a world of need to a world of plenty. Psychologists recognize a resistance to change. This immobility and preference for the status quo causes such a person to consider the new events as a threat and they attempt to sweep them under the table.

We will assume that you are not such a person, or you would not have this book in your hands. We will also assume that nobody with a consciousness of plenty would want to move to a consciousness of need, and that what is now being awaited are the steps you are to take to implement your choice.

Here are those steps. No life trauma. Just pleasant thoughts.

A Simple Procedure to Cause a Shift in Consciousness from Poverty to Plenty

The Hawaiian kahunas, or wise men, knew the power of the mind. They called a level of mind beyond the conscious level the "*unihipili.*" They considered it the Creator within us, the Creator that fills all space and is all-intelligent. Since there is no written source for this, we must rely on those whose research has become most respected and used by Hawaiians today. Such an authority is the late Mary Fukui, who calls the *unihipili* a "kind of spiritual pipeline to supernatural powers." The Druids must have known of this pipeline, too. Their "magic" transcended sleight of hand and optical illusion and manifested quite dramatically in material ways.

A breed of New Age scientists today has endorsed this concept and developed ways to harness this spiritual pipeline for personal gain. Conventional scientists have turned their professional backs on inner knowledge obtained subjectively.

A strong bias exists against all knowledge that has not been obtained and tested by standard measurable procedures.

Meanwhile, millions of people, encouraged by their spiritual beliefs or trained by such commercial courses as the Silva Method, are able to tap this supernatural power within through simple relaxation accompanied by special mental communication.

You have already followed the simple step to relax the body and mind outlined in Chapter 1. Prepare now to learn the simple steps that enable you to communicate with the supernatural power within you that we have been calling the Creator.

It is something that has been considered a waste of time. It is forbidden in the conventional classroom. Yet it is the most powerful attribute of the human mind.

It is called daydreaming.

A Similarity Between Nightdreaming and Daydreaming

The encephalogram measures brain pulsations. These pulsations are electrical waves that are a measure of states of consciousness.

Right now, your brain waves are probably at a frequency of 14 to

22 per second. If you were to close your eyes and relax, chances are you would lower your brain wave frequency to somewhere between seven and 14 waves per second.

That is called the alpha brain wave frequency. It is at the alpha brain wave frequency that we daydream. It is also at the alpha brain wave frequency that we dream at night.

The active brain wave frequency you are now at is called beta. We start to fall asleep below alpha, at four to seven pulsations per second, called theta, and as our brain waves slow up to below four, at delta, we are in deep sleep.

We do not dream at delta. We do not dream at theta. But during the night, every hour and a half our brain waves become faster and, when they reach alpha, we begin to dream.

These periodic nightdreams have something in common with daydreams. They often turn out to be inspired by the source of infinite intelligence we call the Creator.

Niels Bohr, a physicist who worked for years to discover the nature of matter, received the information he needed to construct the periodic table of elements in a dream. That dream won him the Nobel Prize. The Nobel Prize is, besides the honor, real money. His dream made him rich.

So did a dream of Sir Frederick Grant Banting, who discovered in a dream his laboratory approach for production of insulin. The biographers of Giuseppe Tartini, composer of "The Devil's Sonata," describe how it came to him in a nightdream. In the dream, he handed his violin to the devil to see how he could play. "I heard him play with consummate skill a sonata of such exquisite beauty... I felt enraptured." He awoke, picked up his violin, and tried to play the sounds he heard in the dream. The piece he then composed was not as good as he heard in his dream, but it was still the best he had ever done.

Robert Louis Stevenson exploited his dreams in his notable writing career. An example was *Dr. Jekyll and Mr. Hyde*, where a difficult part of the plot—the transformation—came to Stevenson in a dream. This was when Hyde, in the presence of his pursuers, took the powder and underwent the change to Dr. Jekyll.

These nightdreams have something in common with daydreams. They are both the source of creativity. Nightdreams are more spontaneous. Daydreams are more under control and purposeful. Each foreshadows reality.

Mary marveled at what a beautiful day it was and wished she could take her children to the beach. But she did not have any money, not even bus fare. She relaxed and daydreamed about being at the beach and helping the children play in the sand.

A few minutes later, one of her boys came running in. "Hey, Mom, look what we found on the lawn!" It was a ten-dollar bill.

What is there about nightdreams and daydreams that make them both creative?

They are both at the alpha level.

CHAPTER 7 -- FROM "THE COMPLETE BOOK OF LIFE-CHANGING AFFIRMATIONS"

"The word is still a creative power. This book gives you words to use that can create a new world for you," Stone wrote. It includes 200 positive affirmations to help visualize your goals and activate the mind's energy to achieving them. Here is one.

Read this affirmation several times until you can recite it by memory. Reciting it by memory does not have to be perfect; in fact, substituting your own words can enhance the results because you are making it more personal.

Sit in a comfortable chair. Close your eyes. Take a nice deep breath. Sit quietly a few moments being aware of your normal breathing. Mentally affirm the words to yourself. Do this three times. Mentally picture yourself living up to the affirmation. In other words, daydream about its coming to be so.

Do this daily ....

Acquiring More Money

I release all past memories of poverty and need. They are exceptions to the abundance that is natural in this world. I how have expectations of plenty. Abundance is my legacy. ("See" yourself living a more abundant life). Wealth now comes to me in many forms.

I have a consciousness of plenty. Past periods of scarcity are errors in my own expectations. My consciousness of plenty is creative of plenty. I attract all that I need to survive in style. ("See" yourself living in style).

Money is energy. I desire, expect, and believe that more and more energy is entering my life and that money is one of its common forms. I see a blizzard of bills blowing at me (See a snowstorm of hundred dollar bills surrounding you). I am richer and richer every day.

As I receive, I give. I am an open channel for Nature's wealth. It flows through me without limit as I use it for the good of myself, my business, my family, and the family of man. There is limitless wealth on the way.

All that I have is a gift from the Creator. Because I have a commitment to serve the Creator, His gifts to me are boundless. I listen to Him and attempt to do His Will.

I become a better and better channel for His infinite wealth. Universal life energy and wealth surges through me as I go forth.

CHAPTER 8 -- FROM "THE SILVA MIND CONTROL METHOD FOR BUSINESS MANAGERS"

In this book, José Silva and Robert B. Stone focus on harnessing the Silva Method for success in business. Excerpts below are examples of what managers can do at the alpha level to tap into intuition and the subjective dimension to take themselves, their teams, and their organizations to new levels of achievements.

From Success to Failure

Man loses job. Man becomes depressed. Man is overwhelmed by a sense of failure. Man separates himself from re1atives and friends. Depression deepens. Interviews fail. Man claims, "I'm a loser." Sound familiar?

It happens every day—but not when you learn the Silva Method. And it need never happen to you once you train yourself according to the procedures in this book. The Silva Method puts you in charge of your mind. You understand all the positive aspects of yourself. As you begin to "push the positive buttons," you begin identifying with success. You transfer positive energy, or feeling, to others. You light up in their eyes as a winner.

B.A., twenty-four, of Florida, got a job in the space program at Cape Kennedy. He was proudly realizing the dream of his youth. But, within a year, he was out. It was a blow. He had not saved any money. His feeling of pride turned to a feeling of inferiority. He heard about the Silva Method. He had to borrow the tuition money from a friend.

He began using what he learned immediately to program himself to find a job. Within one week he was working. It was not an ideal job, but it enabled him to save money during his first year with that company. He enjoyed making waterbeds. He used the money to buy waterbed materials. Now he used his Silva Method training to "see" himself in the waterbed business. He went to his Alpha level of mind for two or three minutes every day and "saw" himself conducting a waterbed business successfully.

First, he manufactured the beds at night in his home and sold them on weekends. Soon he had to rent a vacant store. He still worked weekdays at his job, programmed daily, and made profitable sales on Saturdays and Sundays. Within one more year he had two full-time stores and was well on his way to grossing a million dollars a year.

B.A.'s story is not sensational, but it is typical of everyday uses to which the Silva Method is being put by countless businesspeople. These businesspeople do not fill unemployment offices, bankruptcy courts, or hospitals; they fill bank accounts.

If our friend B.A. is the microcosm, here is the macrocosm.

From Night into Day

The NDM Corporation, located on the Miami River in Dayton, Ohio, manufactures machines used in the medical field and also develops plastics for use within the human body. Its president took the Silva Method training course and decided to have all 550 employees trained.

The training course started with eighty employees at a time, most of whom were at management levels. In one of the first classes was a chemist working to find a new plastic that the body would not reject and that could be used for arteries in bypass surgery. This chemist decided to use a Silva Method technique that puts the mind to work on a problem while you are asleep.

He awoke during the night with a vivid recollection of a dream about a formula. He wrote it down. When he examined the formula at the plant in the morning, it was almost identical to one he had already tried with negative results. "Why waste time," a colleague said, "we have already worked on that one." But he had a gut feeling that the small difference in the formula might make a big difference. Over the objections of his colleague, he put together a sample, tested it, and it worked!

When we dream, the mind comes up from deep levels of sleep to the Alpha level. At the Alpha level, the mind is capable of obtaining solutions in genius-like ways. Answers are brought from the darkness of the unconscious to the light of day.

Prosperity Starts in the Subjective Dimension

With no formal education, I (José Silva) was successful and prosperous all my life and in all areas of my life. There are many sides to prosperity: your health can prosper; so can your relationships with family or colleagues. We can experience a rich joy in living. We can have a storehouse of memories of problems solved and people served. We can have all the money we need.

Most people equate prosperity with material success—money. However, as important as the money is, it cannot be fully enjoyed without good health, or if you have family problems or your work is boring.

To attain prosperity in its fullest sense, we need clairvoyance, confidence, enthusiasm, and work.

Read that sentence again. "Fullest sense" means not only the money but the health and opportunity to enjoy prosperity. And the word "clairvoyance" seems to add a strange dimension to the three standard ingredients that appear in all the classic texts.

I once appeared as a speaker on the same rostrum with W. Clement Stone, head of a major insurance organization and author of several successful "success" books. He has accumulated great wealth and teaches his employees and others his method. I listened and watched, I could see that W. Clement Stone is a natural clairvoyant, who learned to use and trust his intuition at an early age. I am also a clairvoyant. It takes one to know one.

What is a clairvoyant? It is a person who "receives" information beyond the range of his eyes or senses, a person who intuitively "sees" decisions and solutions in a way that appears to be guesswork, but that proves to be accurate and dependable.

Who is a clairvoyant? Everybody is. You are. When your eyes are closed you cannot see. When you are closed to clairvoyance, you cannot be intuitive. The objective work-a-day world of living has a way of closing us to clairvoyance, because clairvoyance functions under our control only at the subjective level.

With the Silva Method, as explained in the pages ahead, you learn to function at the subjective level when the need arises. You learn to find and use your clairvoyance.

As you practice, you build confidence. Confidence activates expectancy and enthusiasm. Then, the work flows easily, joyfully, and prosperity is manifested.

This material world springs from energy. Destroy the atom and it returns to that energy form. Energy is cause. Material is effect. The energy of our consciousness is at this causal, creative level. When we withdraw from the objective world mentally, and go to the subjective level, we are using our mental energy in a causal, creative dimension.

If you need something in the objective world, you can set the creative wheels in motion at the subjective dimension. This is the activation of clairvoyance. This is the beginning of prosperity. This is the way of the super manager.

Welcome to the subjective dimension.

The Source of Genius

Economic pressures have sometimes forced people to look for supplemental sources of income. Then these supplemental sources surprisingly surpass the main source and become the full-time business.

It is as if an intelligence greater than our own was involved in the circumstances; perhaps the same intelligence that made my friend's programming for a raise result in the loss of his job so he could be offered a better job; perhaps the same intelligence that drove a Malaysian bank auditor to quit a lucrative position without a new one to step into, only to earn a $250,000 finder's fee a week later.

When I programmed for a dream to help me solve my money problem and dreamt of numbers that turned out to be a winning lottery ticket, I had a distinct feeling that I was not the genius, that some other genius was at work.

Can we take credit for intuition? Or does it come from a source outside of ourselves? We can take credit for our education, our learning, our experience, and for the ability to apply these to problems and circumstances. But can we take credit for unexplained perception, ESP, clairvoyance, psychic ability?

Enter Higher Intelligence.

One day we will understand better why putting the objective dimension on "hold" and activating the subjective mind gives us access to Higher Intelligence. In fact, it might take that Higher Intelligence for us to acquire that understanding.

Those who are satisfied to work at the objective level, as they are now, and take home that paycheck regularly may be enjoying a false sense of security. Life has a way of jolting the comfortable status quo.

"I don't need my subjective realm," they say. "Oh, yeah?" says life.

Access to Higher Intelligence is available for us for a reason. The reason can only be that we need it.

CHAPTER 9 -- FROM "CELESTIAL 911"

In "Celestial 911," Robert B. Stone teaches controlled "daydreaming" as a technique to open life's doors through the portal of the mind. He uses the metaphor of a guardian angel as a tool to focus the imaginative powers of the mind. He guides readers "through your imaginary doorway into the realm of magic" to see a "fairyland scene of glittering spires, golden domes, and sparkling steeples." One such building is the "Universal Bank" which has access to all the wealth of the universe.

Money is the symbol of abundance. The flow of money into and out of people's lives is probably, next to love, their greatest concern. This concern yields a strange situation: the rich get richer and the poor get poorer. This was recognized even as far back as the writing of the Bible.

Can you understand this apparent unfairness now? A poor man daydreams about his lack and pictures a difficult tomorrow. Since daydreams are creative, the poor man's worrisome daydreams are perpetuating his lack. Meanwhile, the rich man is having different daydreams. He is counting his money and imagining all the things he will be doing with his growing wealth. So the rich man is perpetuating and increasing his abundance through creative daydreaming.

The energy of consciousness is real energy. It is called psychotronic energy. When you relax and daydream, you focus your psychotronic energy on the subject of your mental images. This is creative energy.

So you tend to create what you picture mentally.

Start now to eliminate worry, pessimism, and other negativity from your relaxed thoughts. You are getting in your own way....

Imagining a doorway is a static act. It just stands there. Closed. You need to imagine it opening, visualize help coming, and see your needs being met. All that is far from static. It is dynamic. It is action.

I will be giving you instructions throughout this book for using your imagination dynamically to get help from guardian angels and good fairies. I call these instructions Action Plans.

Each Action Plan will not only open the doorway to obtaining help for you but it will bring that help through the doorway and into your life.

Walter needed three thousand dollars to pay back mortgage payments or he risked losing his house. With a wife and three elementary school children, such a loss was unthinkable. I recommended an Action Plan to help him. When he read it, Walter agreed that the Action Plan seemed to fit his financial problem, and he put the instructions down and followed them. In about two minutes, he had completed it. He opened his eyes. No, no genie stood in front of him with three thousand dollars. The room was the same. In fact, for two weeks nothing at all happened except his time to pay the mortgage arrears was running out.

At the end of those two weeks, his wife decided to clean the attic. It was piled with old boxes, memorabilia, and endless photo albums left by her parents. As she thumbed through the albums, curious as to who were in the photos, she came across an album not with photos but with postage stamps. Apparently one of her parents had been a stamp collector. Neither she nor her husband was interested in acquiring this hobby, so they took the album to a professional philatelist in order to cash in on what little the stamp collection might be worth. They left with three thousand five hundred dollars!

Was it a miracle that saved their house? Or a good fairy?

YOUR FIRST ACTION PLAN: HOW TO COME INTO EXTRA MONEY

This Action Plan manifests extra money for you quite speedily.

Read these instructions over a couple of times until they become familiar to you. A friend or relative who is of like mind with you may read the step-by-step procedure to you as you do it, but it is better if you proceed alone.

Prepare your mental state. Wash away all feelings of financial limitation. Prepare yourself mentally to accept unlimited abundance. Practice relaxing according to the steps provided earlier. Also practice daydreaming using the steps provided here in this book. Once you are comfortable with the procedures for relaxing and using your imagination, follow the steps in this Action Plan if you are in need of some extra money.

Action Plan for Extra Money

1. Relax.

2. Daydream.

3. Mentally open the doorway and walk in.

4. State firmly that you need more money.

5. Ask for help.

6. Place on your lap a dollar bill or higher denomination that you have collected in preparation for this Action Plan.

7. With your eyes still closed, visualize a ball of light about a foot over your head. Turn up the brilliance of the light. Permit the ball of brilliant light to slowly descend into your

head, sinking slowly down your body until it reaches the level of your solar plexus (just above the navel). Now shine a beam of light out your navel and onto the money. See the money become aglow with energy. Turn off the beam. Imagine the money going out and away. Wait a moment. Now see a shower of money returning. See the air filled with countless returning bills. Slowly return the ball of light up your body and out of your head to the point above your head where it started. Dim the light of the ball. Imagine you are walking out the doorway and back to your chair; leave the door open. Open your eyes.

8. Spend the bill or change it within twenty-four hours.

HOW TO KEEP MONEY FLOWING TO YOU

Do you have a skill or talent that is proving to be a valuable asset to you? Have you ever helped others to develop a similar talent?

As a musician, author, poet, or artist, do you feel that by helping another person to get started in your field, you are increasing the competition, which is already stiff?

Here's the answer via a story. A young couple signed a lease in a new community shopping center for their new shoe store. Business was terrible. They were financed adequately to last out those first six months to a year, which any new business must be prepared to do. But at the end of a year, they were a long way from making a living.

When they heard that two vacant stores in the shopping center were also just leased to shoe companies, they threw their hands up. This was the last straw. How could three businesses show a profit when even one was in the red? They decided to relocate.

While they were looking for another site for their shoe business, a funny thing began to happen. The other stores had opened and now their own store began to thrive. They realized that where their own store attracted only a few shoe customers, three shoe stores attracted ten times as many shoe customers. Moral: The more the merrier.

I have assisted many would-be authors to become published authors. And my royalties rose. The same can be true for any gifted person who helps another to develop a similar talent.

Are you exporting? Show me how. Are you franchising? Show me how. Are you advertising successfully? Show me how.

One rule: Don't ask me, or whomever you help, for money. Do your sharing without a fee.

Since I or the person you help does not pay you, the universe must pay you. There is no way to be creative, productive, or helpful without your receiving your just reward. Since recipients are not taking care of you, the universe automatically takes care of you.

And the universe pays much higher than union wage.

If you do not have a special talent, skill, or ability to share with others, all is not lost. There are many simple ways to help others.

Depending on the substantiality of your sharing, you may receive surprise gifts. Lisa received a valuable antique from an aging collector she assisted. Andrew won a lottery after he helped a family to move.

Or, good things may happen to you, a sort of serendipity. A long-forgotten loan may be repaid. Or you may receive an unexpected tax refund. Or an uncle whom you never really knew may bequeath a sizable sum.

Consider these all as payments to you by the universe, through the Universal Bank, for value received.

There is nobody whom you can help that is outside this universal reciprocity.

We are all one.

Printed in Great Britain
by Amazon

80602381R00058